URBANIZATION IN NORTHEAST INDIA
Issues and Concerns

Urbanization in Northeast India

Issues and Concerns

Edited by
H. Sudhir

AKANSHA PUBLISHING HOUSE
NEW DELHI - 110002 (INDIA)

AKANSHA PUBLISHING HOUSE
4649-B,Ansari Road,
Daryaganj, New Dellii-11 0002
Phones:23268193, 9811582579, 09435116718
Email: ektabooks@yahoo.com
visit us: www.akanshapublishinghouse.com

Urbanization in Northeast India: Issues and Concerns

First Published 2009

ISBN 978-81-8370-192-1

PRINTED IN INDIA

Published by Akansha Publishing House, New Delhi-110002 and printed at Mehra Offset Press, Delhi.

Contents

Preface

Urbanization and development complementarily reinforce each other. Urbanization is seen as an integral force of development and vice versa. The process of urbanization is the growth in terms of the proportion of population living in the urban areas, which is intimately associated with the transformation in economic activities followed by changes in socioeconomic spheres and development of human social productivity.

The northeast region has been experiencing a trend of upswing urbanization in terms of unprecedented proliferation of towns and high level of urbanization but the pattern of urbanization almost seems to be unaccompanied by perceptible shift in economic organization, commensurated industrialization of productive activities and expansion of necessary urban amenities. In addition, the pattern of the growth of urbanization has given birth to a host of emerging problems that is inseparably tied up with the type of undergoing urbanization process in the region.

Though urbanization process is rather a recent phenomenon, its pace of growth in the recent decades is quite fast. But, haphazard planning or lacking of proper urban management breeds a bunch of urban problems like overcrowding, growth of slums, scarcity of water-supply, inadequate public health and sanitation (e.g. laboratories are katcha types and unhygienic), raising unemployment among the youth, poverty, unplanned drainage system (e.g. water logging during the rainy summer is common phenomenon and drainages are mostly katcha types), unhygienic piled up garbages, socio-economic and political problems and on. The problem of urbanization is inextricably knotted to the inadequacies of legislative enactments, ineffectiveness in the functioning of the municipal and the local bodies in urban civic management, ad hoc urban development schemes etc.

Contrary to the conventional understanding of urbanization for a requisite to development, urbanization in this less developed peripheral territory of India's northeast has brought 'spurious consumerism' and distorted development instead of generating improved productive capacities.

The emerging problem of urbanization is now a subject matter of considerable debate for the policy makers, administrators and academicians. A meaningful alleviation of the urban problems depends on an integrated strategy involving appropriate policy making, effective administrative machinery, responsive academic contribution and strengthened community participation. Every urban citizen's access to minimum basic urban amenities is dependent on the state's urban policy initiatives. Shouldering this responsibility, various urban schemes and planning for the people living in the urban areas under the overall development process have been initiated though benefited inadequately hence an integrated alternative strategy specific to the regional- contextual urban problems is necessarily called forth. Despite the government's initiatives to respond effectively to the problem, there are problems in functioning or implementation of the programmes and the absence of built-in capacity for designing the appropriate intervention to suit the problem. Another crucial issue affecting in pragmatic and uniform implementation of the urban policy lies in the dichotomy of cooperative partnership between the urban management of the government and the people's insensitivity towards maintaining civic urban way of life. The need for an appropriate institutional framework for implementing urban management programme touching several aspects viz, state, non-governmental organizations, institutions of civil society and community participation is felt to ensure maximum efficiency of urban management aimed at providing basic urban amenities. The need is to encourage an integrated participatory approach in planning, implementing, and managing feasible productive urban policies linked to the specific regional infrastructural requirements.

Sensing the seriousness and importance of the problem, the present work intends to go into the depth of understanding the crux of the problem. Specifically, the work designs to touch upon the meaning, extent, dynamics, problems and overall impact of urbanization in the region.

The present work has originated from a workshop *Problems, Prospects and Patterns of Urbanization in Manipur* organized by the Ereima Gender Empowerment & Resource Centre under the financial support of the Indian Council of Social Science Research (ICSSR), New Delhi in 2005. These are all modified and revised versions of the papers presented in the workshop. Meanwhile, papers submitted are also incorporated. All the paper contributors are appreciated for their support and co-operation.

It has been my pleasure editing the volume. For support and cooperation, gratitude is extended to H. Jubita, Bhavina Sharma, S. Bimol, H. Sureshkumar, Bimol Hajarimayum and Sundari. Words are not enough to express my thanks to M.P. Misra for his constant encouragement to arrive the book in this present shape. I thank him for publishing this volume.

The editor laid hands in editing task yet neither the editor nor the Centre nor the publisher claims the responsibility of the papers. Views expressed in the papers are entirely of the authors concerned.

—H. Sudhir

Our Contributors

Amar Yumnam, Professor, Economics, Manipur University, Imphal

Dharmendra Nath, Lecturer, Economics, Goalpara College, Assam

Dr. Nissar A Barua, Lecturer, Economics Gauhati University, Assam

H.C Gautam, Reader, Commerce, Gauhati University, Assam

Indraneel Bhowmick, Assistant Professor, Economics Women's College, Agartala, Tripura

Jiten Yumnam, Citizen's Concern for Dams and Development, Manipur

Kalyan Das, Omeo Kumar Das Institute of Social Change and Development, Dispur, Assam

K. Meghachandra Singh, Research Scholar, History, Manipur University

M. Manas Singh, Junior Town Planner Town Planning Department, Government of Manipur

Purushottam Bhandari, Sr. Lecturer, Economics, Jagiroad College, Assam

U.A. Shimray, Institute for Social and Economic Change, Bangalore

1

Urbanization in Manipur: From Soft Underbelly of Development to Fiercest Agendum

Amar Yumnam

Introduction

As we all know, we follow the census definition of urban area, and on it we generally base our discussions of urbanization. This has the advantage of comparability over time and space. But this is not what I would like to dwell on. I would rather be concerned with the political economy aspects of the urban phenomenon in Manipur.

Nevertheless, for the sake of convenience, let me reproduce below some statistics that might be repeated in various papers in the Workshop.

Issues

The figures (Table 1.1) throw up some interesting issues. They are:

1. The urbanization process in Manipur has followed rather a pattern of arrested or stunted growth. This is evident from the lack of growth in the ratios during the last three Censuses.

Table 1.1
Urban Population Ratio of Manipur

Census Year	Urban population ratio to total population		
	Persons	*Male*	*Female*
1901	25.40	25.41	25.37
1911	21.56	21.32	21.79
1921	20.83	20.34	21.31
1931	19.26	18.61	19.87
1941	19.47	19.04	19.88
1951	0.5	0.62	0.38
1961	8.68	8.82	8.55
1971	13.19	13.19	13.19
1981	26.42	26.45	34.79
1991	27.52	27.48	27.56
2001	23.88	23.51	24.25

2. Secondly, the gender figures are uniquely interesting. Unlike urban centres elsewhere where male proportion exceeds female proportion, the ratio of urban women exceeds male ratio in six of the last eleven censuses covering a century. This must be a reflection of the active participation of women in the economic affairs, particularly market processes, in the State.

These are some of the issues, which need to be examined in the context of pattern of overall macro growth of the economy. I would, however, like everyone to go beyond these conventional approaches of urban analysis. In other words, my plea is for appreciating the urbanization phenomena in the State from three contextual realities. They are:

(a) The distinctiveness of the urbanization process in the State as different from the urbanization processes in global development history;

(b) The ethnic plurality of the State; and

(c) The conflict situation in the State.

Let me try to elaborate on these three; all these have connected dynamics and implications. First, allow me to explain what I mean by distinctiveness of the urban phenomenon in the State. Here I am reminded of the analysis of the causes of opulence in the *Inquiry in to the Nature and Causes of the Wealth of Nations.* This is but the relationship between manufacturing and urban growth. Though there have been shifts in the importance of urban centres according to emerging and shifting importance of different manufacturing items, the relationship between manufacture and urban growth has been unequivocal. Even this historical relationship has undergone transformation in the sense of a divorce between manufacturing and urban growth since the adoption of structural adjustment programmes around the globe from about the 1980s. This historical pattern is observable across the globe from Pittsburg to Glasgow to Mumbai.

But urbanization in the State is absolutely different from this stylized scenario. The urban centres in the State are basically administrative centres. So, urban centres in the State are— (a) fundamentally centres for worshipping government, and (b) platforms for political competitions rather than centres for development transformation. We should remember the historical role of urban centres as sources of technological change and ultimately of economic growth anywhere else in the world. We can take up any sectoral issue, like health, education or infrastructure, and the peculiarity of our urbanization would immediately become visible. These definitely have had deleterious implications for the multi-ethnic society like ours. The situation has further had both causal and effect relationships for the conflict atmosphere in the State.

The Implications

The most disturbing implication of the urbanization process in the State is the inability so far of it to take the whole State along. First, the market penetration and social change has been very limited in space and community categories. Secondly, the market process has failed to monetise the economy for an effective modern exchange. This, one may say a blessing in disguise, is evident from the non-collapse of the economy despite the various blows to the polity. In other words, in Manipur we find an absolute lack of connectivity between overall economic growth and urbanization process in the State.

The results emerging from the various rounds of economic censuses convey equally disturbing picture. We find a declining growth rate of non-agricultural enterprises and declining employment-intensity of these enterprises, though there has been no rise in capital-intensity. This implies that the few enterprises we have got in our urban areas lack dynamicity.

All these failures of our urban centres have had their telling effect in terms of the deepening ethnic divide in the State. If we appreciate this in the context of (a) non-falling transportation costs; and (b) dangerously rising political transaction costs of any policy or programme, one will definitely lose one's sleep. Further, all these are happening in an economy where urbanization has been founded on agglomeration economies arising out of production, but rather on political conveniences.

Here we are made to strongly miss the Manipur of 1950s and 1960s when the state enjoyed a high level of social capital, high level of community and individual initiatives for public goods and very low level of political transaction costs. But cumulative administration and governance failures and institutional and political lapses have made all these dissipated. It is in such atmosphere that urbanization has turned into a fiercest agendum from the earlier soft underbelly of development. But the pattern of worshipping government has not led to the emergence of any coherent policy for development intervention. People now worship government for enhancing personal benefits or reducing damages, whereas this is not governed by any logical or coherent policy. So this has led to the high incidence and rising density of corruption in an atmosphere of rising political transaction costs. While political competition had led to Schumpeterian innovation in Europe and the United States, political fragmentation in Manipur has not had any positive impact on development milieu.

We are encountering all this when the current thinking about urban and city planning has moved away from the *Age of Master Plans* to the *Age of Consensus.* The challenge of urban research is indeed gigantic and unique in our State. But the rewards both socially and academically would be even greater.

2

Patterns of Population and Urbanization in Manipur

U.A. Shimray

[Abstract

Manipur state is topographically divided into two features viz., Hills and Valley. The state population comprises a vast mosaic of numerous ethnic groups. The decadal growth rate during 1981-1991 is recorded 29 per cent, however, in the latest population census, the growth rate is recorded 18 per cent considerably declined as compared to the previous decade. Among the population the tribal account 34 per cent. The urban situation in Manipur is depended on the continuation of notified and de-notified towns. Many towns are de-notified due to non-fulfillment of urban concept. In the last three census years there is no significant change in the proportion of urban population in Manipur. However, in the hill areas, there is a drastic change in the proportion. The prevailing social and economic disparity between the hill and valley areas is a serious issue. To narrow down the inter-regional disparities, there should be balanced economic investment and adequate social development.]

Introduction

History without geography is like a picture without frame. For an intelligent understanding of the pattern of development of society and culture, one should begin with the geographical factors (Subba Rao, 1958). Geography, as one of the discipline of social sciences shares close frontier with other social sciences. The geography continues to be neglected by most branches of social sciences. Among the branches of geography, population and urbanisation are directly interrelated with the developmental process and have close correlation.

North Eastern region of India manifests interesting geographical features as well as social and cultural system and demographic settings. Tiny Manipur state situated in the eastern part of the region lies in between 92°58'East and 94°45'East longitudes and 23°50'North and 25⁰42'North latitudes in the Indo-Myanmar frontier. Almost bottle-shaped and landlocked Manipur has an area of 22,327 sq. km. having two distinct topographic features; the Hill ranges that surrounding the central plains known as Imphal valley. The valley measures only 2,238 sq. km. whereas the hills account 20,089 sq. km. Manipur shares boundaries with Nagaland State on the north, *Somra* hills and Upper Chindwin river of Myanmar on the east, Chin Hills (Myanmar) and Mizoram state on the south and Cachar Hills district of Assam on the west.

Administratively, the state is divided into 9 [Nine] districts. The hilly districts are (1) Senapati, (2) Churachandpur, (3) Chandel, (4) Ukhrul, and (5) Tamenglong. The valley area consist of four districts: (1) Thoubal, (2) Bishnupur (3) Imphal East and (4) Imphal West [In 2001 the Imphal district was divided into two districts namely Imphal East and Imphal West]. The districts are further divided into sub-divisions. There are altogether 38 [thirty eight] sub-divisions. The valley areas have 14 [fourteen] and 24 [twenty-four] in the hills.

In this paper, I shall attempt to examine the population scenario, trend of urbanisation and its developmental implications in Manipur. The analysis is based on the quantitative secondary data and relevant documents.

Manipur: Peopling

The state comprises a vast mosaic of numerous ethnic groups. Broadly, the population is categorised as Non-tribal

Table 2.1
Manipur Total Population and Growth Rate

	Total Population			*Decadal Growth Rate*	
State/District	*1971*	*1981*	*1991*	*1971-81*	*1981-91*
Manipur	10,72,753	14,20,953	18,37,149	32.46	29.29
Hill Districts	3,48,216	4,91,876	6,51,157	41.25	32.38
Senapati	1,04,175	1,55,421	2,08,406	49.19	34.09
Tamenglong	44,975	62,289	86,278	38.50	38.51
Churachandpur	98,114	1,34,776	1,76,184	37.37	30.72
Ukhrul	62,229	82,946	1,09,275	33.29	31.74
Chandel*	38,723	56,444	71,014	45.76	25.81
Valley Districts	7,24,537	9,29,077	11,85,992	28.23	27.65
Thoubal	-	2,31,781	2,93,958	-	26.83
Bishnupur	-	1,41,150	1,80,773	-	28.07
Imphal	-	5,56,146	7,11,261	-	27.89
Imphal**	7,24,537	9,29,077	11,85,992	28.23	27.65

Notes: * In 1971, the district was part of Manipur Central District. Chandel district includes Tengnoupal, Chandel and Chakpikarong sub-divisions.

** Including Thoubal and Bishnupur districts [After 1981 census, the Manipur Central district is divided into three districts namely, Thoubal, Bishnupur and Imphal].

Source: Office of the Registrar General and Census Commissioner. 1971, 1981 & 1991. *Series-14 Manipur, Final Population Totals.* New Delhi: Office of the Registrar General and Census Commissioner.

[General], Scheduled Tribes and Scheduled Castes. The indigenous inhabitants of Manipur belong to the *Mongoloid* stock speaking *Tibeto-Burman* languages. Ethnic groups inhabiting the state can be categorised as: the hill communities and the valley-based communities. The valley communities are the *Meiteis* and the *Pangan* [Muslim]. They are recognised as non-tribal. The Government of India recognised 29 [twenty-nine] ethnic groups as Scheduled Tribes [according to 1991 population census]. The tribal groups further categorised as the *Nagas* and the *Kuki-Chin-Zomi.* The recognised ethnic groups as STs are *Anal, Angami, Chiru, Chothe, Kabui, Kacha Kacha Nagas, Koireng, Koirao, Lamkang,*

Mao, Maram, Maring, Monsang, Moyon, Sema, Zou, Vaiphei, Simte, Paite, Purum, Aimol, Gangte, Thadou, Tangkhul, Suhte, Ralte, Kom, Any Mizo [Lushai] and *Hmar*. Indeed, Manipur state presents remarkable sociocultural and linguistic diversity.

Table 2.1 indicates the population scenario of Manipur. In 1991 population census, Manipur recorded a total population of 18,37,149 persons. The decadal growth rate during the decade 1971-1981 is 32.46 per cent. However, the growth rate is marginally declined in 1981-1991 with 29.29 per cent. Among the districts, the Churachandpur, Senapati and Chandel are found to have declined in considerable rate but in other districts, the rate of decline is marginal. In the 1981-1991, the decadal growth rate is found considerably higher in the hills than the valley.

Population 2001 Imbroglio [Exclusion of Mao-Maram, Paomata and Purul Sub-divisions of Senapati District]

The population census of India's *"Provisional Population Totals"* published on April 2001 records the Manipur state's total population as 23, 88,634 persons. After two years gap, the Office of the Registrar General and Census Commissioner, India released the *"Final Population Totals"* on May 2004. In final population, Manipur state recorded total population 21, 66,788 persons [The figure excludes the population of *Mao-Maram, Paomata* and *Purul* Sub-divisions of Senapati district]. The population of Mao-Maram, Paomata and Purul Sub-divisions appeared in Census of India's Provisional Population Totals were cancelled. The reasons given are "administrative" and "technical" problems.

The table 2.2 shows the total population of Manipur according to Final Population Totals (200 I). An absolute number difference between the "Provisional figure" and "Final" figure of Manipur is 2,21,846 persons [Excluding the figure of *Mao-Maram, Paomata* and *Purul]*. The difference is also observed among the nine districts. In the final population, the valley based districts show increase in number except the Thoubal district, which is reduced by 2,20 I. However, in hill areas there is less population.

In the latest decade (1991-2001), the decadal growth rate is considerably declined as compared to the previous decade (1981-1991). Among the districts, the Chandel recorded the highest with 66.62 per cent. The valley districts including Bishnupur, Imphal and Thoubal are observed much lower growth rate than the hill districts. The Senapati district is recorded a decline of -24.89 per cent excluding the Mao-Maram, Paomata and Purul.

The reason for discarding the data of Mao-Maram, Paomata and Purul sub-division is not indeed a convincing statement. On the other hand, the provisional population of these sub-divisions framing as "controversial census figure" has obvious impression and political gimmick. According to the 2001 population census report, Senapati district particularly Mao-Maram, Paomata and Purul sub-division shows a growth rate of 143.12 per cent in Mao-Maram, Paomata 122.64 per cent and Purul 168.78 per cent. The Senapati district is recorded 81.96. For reference, we can have a logical comparison with the neighbouring state Nagaland. In the decade 1991-2001, the Nagaland state shows a growth rate of 64.41 per cent. Considering Nagaland, the Senapati district and the controversial census figure of three sub-divisions are considerably marginal and have little impact to the state's total population. The fact is the total population based of these sub-divisions is very low.

The Government of India had decided to delimit the Assembly/Parliamentary constituencies in various states based on the population figures according to the latest population census of India. Complaint was lodged to the State regarding the population data of Senapati district. Manipur government conveys the problem to the Registrar General and Census Commissioner and Delimitation Commission that the 2001 population census in some sub-divisions shows "abnormal" growth rate. According to the proposed delimitation, the valley-based districts are going to lose five Assembly Constituencies whereas the hill-based districts will gain five Assembly Constituencies. The Senapati district will be having additional three more Assembly Constituencies and Chandel district and Ukhrul district one each.

Table 2.2: Manipur Total Population, 2001

State/ Districts	*Provisional Population Totals*	*Final Difference Totals*	*Absolute Difference (Provisional and Final Population)*	*Decadal Growth Rate 1991-2001*
Manipur	23,88,634	21,66,788*	(-) 2,21,846	17.94
Hill Districts	*9,83,074*	*7,55,022*	*(-) 2,28,052*	15.95
Senapati	3,79,214	1,56,513*	-	-24.89
Tamenglong	1,11,493	1,11,499	(-) 6	29.23
Churachandpur	2,28,707	2,27,905	(+) 802	29.25
Ukhrul	1,40,946	1,40,778	(-) 168	28.82
Chandel	1,22,714	1,18,327	(-) 4387	66.62
Valley Districts	*14,05,560*	**14,11,766**	*(+) 6206*	*19.03*
Thoubal	3,66,341	3,64,140	(-) 2201	23.87
Bishnupur	2,05,907	2,08,368	(+) 2461	15.26
Imphal West**	4,39,532	4,44,382	(+) 4850	-
Imphal East**	3,93,780	3,94,876	(+) 1096	-
Imphal (include West and East)	8,33,312	8,39,258	(+) 5946	17.99

* Excluding Mao-Maram, Paomata and Purul sub-divisions.

** District created in 2001

Source: (i) Office of the Registrar General and Census Commissioner. 200 I. *Provisional Population Totals*, Series-I India and Series-14 Manipur, Paper-I of 200 I.

(ii) Office of the Registrar General and Census Commissioner. 2001. *Final Population Totals*, Series 1 India, Paper-I of 200 1.

Tribal Population

The Table 2.3 depicts the total tribal population in Manipur state. A proportional share of the tribal population in Manipur records 34.41 in 1991 and 34.2 in 200 I. In the latest population census, the tribal population is recorded highest in Ukhrul (95.53 per cent) followed by Tamenglong, Churachandpur, Chandel, Senapati and the lowest in Imphal [including Thoubal and Bishnupur].

The population figures seemingly involve an abnormality especially the Tamenglong district as the tribal population composition declined from 97.82 per cent to 46.97 per cent from 1971 to 1981 experiencing a negative decadal growth rate - 33.50 per cent [This abnormal figure needs re-examination]. This decline is not at all proportionately distributed in other districts the tribal population share so as to compensate the declined figure.

Conversely, the tribal population increases [decadal growth rate] significantly, almost retaining the 1971 level. Among the districts, highest decadal growth rate is observed in Chandel with 79.12 per cent in 2001 and lowest in Tamenglong and the percentage is 27.62.

Sex Ratio in Manipur

An analysis of sex ratio is presented in the Table 2.4. During 1971 and 1981 the sex ratio was declining in all the hill districts and increasing in all the valley districts. The sex ratio decline was higher than the increase leading to an overall State's ratio to fall during the period 1971-1981. Similarly, the sex ratio declined in all the districts except marginal increase in Senapati and Churachandpur districts which result to a decline in the state's overall sex ratio during 1981-1991. Interestingly, further, the pattern was changed during 1991-200 I by an increase in the ratio in all the districts except Senapati and Tamenglong districts resulting to an overall State's ratio on the rise. In general, the trend was similar in all the valley districts, similar in Chandel and Ukhrul districts, and the rest districts were experiencing a unique trend during the period 1971 to 200 I. Tamenglong's sex ratio has declined rapidly from 1013 females per 1000 males in 1971 to 922 females per 1000 males in 2001.

Sex Ratio among Tribal Population

According to the population census in Manipur for every thousand males there were 1009 females in 1971, 975 females in 1981 and 959 females in 1991 showing steady fall in the sex ratio. This indicates that female population outnumbered by 9 persons in 1971, but the male population outnumbered the

Table 2.3: Total Tribal Population by District-wise

State/District	Total Tribal Population				Decadal Growth Rates (%)			Percentage of Tribal Population to Total Population			
	1971	1981	1991	2001	1971- 81	1981-91	1991- 01	1971	1981	1991	2001
Manipur	334466	387977	632173	741141*	16.00	62.94	17.23	31.18	27.3	34.41	34.2*
Hill Districts	*313102*	363836	585854	684894	*16.20*	*61.02*	*16.90*	89.91	73.96	89.97	*90.71*
Senapati	82706	105655	175206	122791*	27.75	65.82	29.91	79.39	67.97	84.07	78.45*
Tal11eng!ong	43996	29259	83,332	106349	-33.50	184.8	27.62	97.82	46.97	96.59	95.38
Churachandpur	91984	116254	164709	212482	26.39	41.68	29.00	93.75	86.25	93.49	93.23
Ukhrul	59926	74238	101878	134493	23.88	47.3	32.01	96.3	89.5	93.23	95.53
Chandel**	34490	38430	60,729	108779	11.42	58.02	79.12	89.07	68.08	85.52	91.93
Valley Districts	-	-	46319	56247	-	-	21.43	-	-	3.90	3.98
Thoubal	-	-	2,844	4,274	-	-	-	-	-	0.97	1.17
Bishnupur	-	-	9,575	6,143	-	-	-	-	-	5.30	2.94
Imphal ***	-	-	33,900	45,830	-	-	-	-	-	4.77	5.46

Notes: * Excluding Mao-Maram, Paomata and Purul sub-divisions.

** In 1971, the district was part of Manipur Central District. Chandel district includes Tengnoupal, Chandel and Chakpikarong sub-divisions.

*** Including Imphal West and Imphal East.

Source: Office of the Registrar General and Census Commissioner. 1971, 1981, 1991 & 2001. *Series-14 Manipur, Final Population Totals.* New Delhi: Office of the Registrar General and Census Commissioner.

female population by 25 and 41 respectively in 1981 and 1991 among the tribal population. The district wise figure shows a highest sex ratio in Tamenglong with 1057 followed by Chandel, Senapati, Ukhrul, Churachandpur, and the lowest was recorded in Imphal (including Thoubal and Bishnupur districts) with 897 females. In 1981 population census, Tamenglong district recorded the highest sex ratio of 1004 females per one thousand males and is followed by Chandel (984), Senapati (976), Churachandpur (976), Ukhrul (975) and the lowest is recorded in Imphal areas (including Thoubal and Bishnupur district) and the ratio is 919 females. Similarly, Chandel recorded the highest sex ratio at 979 females followed by Churachandpur, Senapati, Tamenglong, Ukhrul, Imphal, Bishnupur and the lowest in Thoubal district at 843 females in 1991 census. The tribal population sex ratio trend is at deteriorating states in all the districts as well as at state level as it declined from 1971 to 1991 except in Imphal where it slightly improved [see Table 2.4].

Table 2.4: Sex Ratio

District/State	*Sex Ratio ofManipur (females per 1000 males)*				*Sex Ratio of Tribal Population in Manipur*		
	1971	*1981*	*1991*	*2001*	*1971*	*/98/*	*1991*
Senapati	949	938	942	923	1013	976	966
Tamenglong	1013	975	935	922	1057	1004	959
Churachandpur	976	929	931	993	1003	976	966
Chandel	975	935	913	985	1026	984	979
Ukhrul	969	917	884	920	1011	975	949
Thoubal	988	994	980	998			843
Bishnupur	981	992	984	1001			853
Imphal East				992			
Imphal West				1007			
Imphal	984	990	973	1000	897*	919*	920
Manipur	980	971	958	978	1009	975	959

* Imphal district figures include for Thoubal and Bishnupur district.
Source: Same as Table 2.3.

Urban Population and Urbanisation

Urbanisation is a process, which reveals itself through temporal, spatial and sectoral changes in demographic, social and economic and environmental aspects. These changes manifest themselves in increasing concentration of population in human settlements larger than villages, in increasing involvement of people in secondary and tertiary activities and also progressive adoption of certain social transition which differ from the traditional rural societies. The urbanisation process is closely linked with the level of development. Most of the developed countries have already achieved a very high level of urbanisation though the process is still unfolding in the developing countries.

Currently, a process of world population growth and urbanisation are found to be closely interlinked. The world's urban population reached 2.9 billion in 2000 and is expected to rise to 5 billion by 2030. From 30 per cent of the world population in urban area in 1950 to 47 per cent by 2000 it is projected to attain 60 per cent by 2030. In the latest Indian population census, the proportion of urban population is recorded 27.81 per cent.

Definition and Concepts: The study of urban phenomena is muddled by a prolific number of concepts, which are frequently and vaguely defined. The United Nations has, therefore recommended the member countries to evolve their own definitions of "urban" on the basis of - (a) Type of local government, (b) Number of inhabitants and (c) Proportion of population engaged in non-agricultural activities.

The United Nations has also suggested that the census results should be tabulated for localities [or other territorial units] according to groups by population size without necessarily specifying which size should be regarded as denoting "urban." India though a developing country has comparatively rich experience in collection and presentation of data in migration and urbanisation through censuses.

Countries differ in the way they classify population as "urban" or "rural." Typically, a community or settlement with a population of 2,000 or more is considered as urban. Urbanisation is the process of growth in the proportion of a population living in urban areas. In India, the definition of 'urban' has remained more or less the same for the period 1901-1951. The definition of urban according to the Census of India (2001) follows as:

(a) All places with a municipality corporation, cantonment board or notified town area committee, etc.

(b) All other places which satisfied the following criteria: a minimum population of 5000, at least 75 per cent of male working population engaged in non-agricultural pursuit and density of population of at least 400 per sq. km.

Table 2.5: Percentage of Urban Population

State/District	*Total Population* 1981	1991	2001
Manipur	26.42	27.52	26.58
Hill Districts	*10.68*	6.65	1.98
Senapati	6.19	00	00
Tamenglong	6.87	00	00
Churachandpur	18.66	19.10	00
Ukhrul	7.02	00	00
Chandel	13.6	13.62	12.64
Valley Districts	34.75	38.98	39.73
Thoubal	-	36.55	36.04
Bishnupur	-	34.94	35.86
Imphal*	-	41.00	42.29

Note: *Including the population of Imphal West district and Imphal East district [In 2001 census, the Imphal district is divided into Imphal East district and Imphal West district].

Source: Same as table 3.

Table 2.5 presents a proportion of urban population in Manipur. Indeed, urban situation in Manipur depends on the continuation of 'notified' and 'de-notified' of town. Many areas/ towns are de-notified due to non-fulfillment of the urban concept and criteria. In the last three census years there is no significant change in the proportion of urban population. However, in the hill areas, there is a drastic change in a proportion. This is due to the de-notification process in the subsequent census years. In the latest population census, a proportion of urban population in hill areas is recorded only 2 per cent [Moreh town of Chandel district is the only available urban area in the hills]. In the valley areas, a proportion of urban popu lation is considerably high accounting 40 per cent.

The Table 2.6 shows the urban population based on social sector. In the latest population census, tribal living in the urban areas is recorded as low as 5 per cent whereas; in non-tribal population is 37 per cent. A low percentage among tribal population is largely attributed by the de-notification of urban areas in the hill districts.

Table 2.6: Urban Population by Population Category

Year	*Urban Population*		*Percentage of Urban Population*	
	Non-Tribal	*Tribal*	*Non-Tribal*	*Tribal*
1991	4,33,002	53;243	37.07	8.43
2001	5,01,504	35,229	36,73	4.75

Source: Same as Table 2.3

Type of Urban Areas

On the basis of the above criteria two distinct types of urban area emerge: (i) a type of towns notified by the tate government under special Acts and is known as statutory towns, (ii) the second type is based on the fulfilment of the demographic criteria stated in urban definition (b) is known as Census Town (CT).

Till 1961, Manipur had only one town namely- Imphal. In the decade 1961-1971, the town *Churachandpur, Thoubal, Kakching, Moirang, Nambol, Bishnupur* and *Lamlai* were notified as statutory towns. Subsequently, more areas were declared as urban centres.

They are: *Mao, Karong, Senapati, Kangpokpi, Tamenglong, Ukhrul, Singhat, Moreh, Heirok, Sikhong Sekmai, Wangjing, Yairipok, Lilong (Thoubal), Sugnu, Lilong (Imphal West), Wangoi, Mayang Imphal, Samurou, Jiribam, Lamsang, Sekmai Bazar, Ningthoukhong, Kumbi* and *Oinam*. However, in 1991 population census, seven towns were denotified while four more new statutory towns and two census towns were added. The total urban areas in 1991 were 31 (thirty-one) in number. In the latest census, *Churachandpur* was declassified as rural areas based on the demographic criteria of urban area (see Table 2.7).

Table 2.7: Size Categories and Number of Urban Centres in Manipur, 2001

Size	*Number of Town*	*Name of the Town*
< 5000	5	Lamlai (NP), Sekmai Bazar (NP), Sugnu (NP), Heirok (NP) and Torban-Kshetrileikai (CT)
5000-9,999	16	Oinam (NP), Kwakta (NP), Kumbi (P), Yairipok (NP), Samurou (NP), Sikhong Sekmai (NP), Wangjing (NP), Kakching Khunou (NP), Lamsang (NP), Lamjaotongba (CT), Naoriya Pakhanglakpa (CT), Wangoi (NP), Jiribam (MCI), Porompat *(CT)*, Andro (NP) and Khongman *(CT)*
10,000-19,999	8	Nambol (MCI), Bishnupur (MCI), Ningthoukhong (NP), Moirang (MCI), Lilong (Thoubal) (NP), Lilong (Imphal West) (NP), Thongkhong Laxmi Bazar (NP) and Moreh (NP)
20,000-49,999	3	Thoubal (MCI), Kakching (MCI) and Mayang Imphal (NP)
50,000-99,999	0	-
100,000	1	Imphal (MCI & *OG)*

MCI - Municipality Council, NP- Nagar Panchayat, CT- Census Town, OG- Out Growth

Workforce Participation

According to Suri *et al.* (1988: I), "[E]conomically active person may be employed, underemployed or unemployed. The persons who are not economically active can be students, rentier, pensioners, beggars, etc. Those who are employed were further classified according to the nature of their job [occupation, industry, status, etc.]." The population Census of India 2001 idefined work [economic activity] as, participation in any economically productive activity with or without compensation, wages or profit. Such participation may be physical and/or mental in nature. Work involves not only actual work but also includes effective supervision and direction of work. It even includes part time help or unpaid work and farm, family, enterprise or in any other economic activity.

Information on work and economic activities of the individual was collected in India right from 1872 population census. However, the concepts and definitions of economic activities underwent changes from time to time, although efforts were made to maintain uniformity and comparability to the extent possible. In the first post-Independence 1951 population census, population was classified of workers and non-workers based on the income-approach and the persons classified as *self-supporting, earning dependants* and *non-earning dependants.* Self-supporting is defined as a person who is in receipt of an income, whether in cash or kind, which is sufficient at least for own maintenance. A non-earning dependant is a person who does not secure any income in cash or kind, and was wholly dependent on the earning of someone else. Earning dependant is a person who secures a regular income but whose income is not sufficient to support him/her.

In 1961 population census, economic activities were collected on the basis of work. "Work" was defined as "any person whose main activity was participation in any economically productive work either by his/her physical or by his/her mental activity." Those persons who worked on anyone of the days during the reference period of one week prior to the date of enumeration will be considered workers if the persons had participated in any activity like trade, profession, service or business. Also, seasonal works like cultivation, livestock keeping, plantation, some types of household industry, etc., which are not carried on throughout the year are also considered work. And the same concept was followed in 1971 population census.

However, in 1981, the criteria of work were based on duration of hours and days [the definition is same as above]. The entire population is divided into three categories; *main workers, marginal workers,* and *non-workers.* The main workers are defined as those who have worked in some economic activity over a period of six months. In other words, main workers are those who have worked for the major part of the year preceding the enumeration. Marginal workers, on the other hand, are those who have worked any time in the year preceding the enumeration but have not worked for the major part of the year. Non-workers are those who have not participated in any gainful enumeration. The categories included under non-workers are namely, housewife, students, dependant, retired persons, beggars and vagrants, inmates of jail and mental institutes.

In the 1991 population census, time criteria regarding engagement in work remained the same in both main workers and marginal workers. Even the definition of work was unchanged, but here the workers include unpaid work on farm or in family enterprises in order to account for women who do not receive any remuneration for work.

The population Census of India classified the main economic activities into nine industrial categories. The nine industries economic activities are as follows: (i) Cultivators, (ii) Agricultural Labourers, (iii) Livestock, Forestry, Fishing, Hunting, Plantations and Orchard and allied activities, (iv) Mining and Quarrying, (v) Manufacturing processing, Servicing and Repairs in—(a) Household industry, (b) Other than household industry, (vi) Constructions, (vii) Trade and Commerce, (viii) Transport, Storage and Communication and (ix) Other Services.

All the nine industrial categories of main workers can be grouped into three economic sectors that is, *Primary, Secondary* and *Tertiary.* In the *Primary Sector* are included the first four categories i.e., Cultivator, Agricultural labourer, Livestock, Forestry,

Fishing, Hunting, Plantation and Orchard and Allied activities, and Mining and Quarrying. The *Secondary Sector* includes Manufacturing, Processing Servicing and Repairs in- (a) Household Industry, and (b) Other than household industry, and Constructions. The *Tertiary Sector* comprises Trade and Commerce, Transport, Storage and Communication, and Other Services. The categorization into three economic sectors is based on the nature of the production process of the commodity or commodities produced in the particular sectors.

The Table 2.8 presents a proportion of population engaged in agricultural sector and non-agricultural sector. In 1991 population census, 39 per cent of the state's total population was registered as main workers. Among the main workers, the proportion engaged in agricultural sector was the highest with 82 per cent in cultivation, 7 per cent as agricultural labourers, and 2 per cent in mining and quarrying. The non-agricultural sector was 30 per cent.

Table 2.8: Proportion in Agricultural Sectors and Non-Agricultural Sectors 1991

	Total Main Workers	*Agricultural Sectors*			*Non-Agriculture Sectors*
		Cultivation	*Agricultural Labourers*	*Mining & Quarrying*	
Manipur	38.55	61.76	6.68	1.51	30.03
Hill District	46.38	81.78	2.24	*0.01*	15.97
Senapati	50.22	88.50	2.00	0.13	9.35
Tamenglong	45.44	87.25	0.77	0.18	11.66
Churachandpur	42.51	77.41	2.65	0.43	19.46
Chandel	48.30	74.19	5.06	0.69	20.03
Ukhrul	44.77	75.02	1.34	0.77	22.86
Valley District	34.25	46.88	9.95	*0.04*	43.13
Thoubal	36.63	63.06	13.69	1.00	22.22
Bishnupur	38.23	55.88	10.71	5.42	27.97
Imphal East	32.29	39.79	10.33	2.07	47.71
Imphal West	32.22	33.79	5.93	2.05	58.21

Source: Same as Table 2.3.

Region-wise, the hills have recorded 46 per cent as main workers in 1991 population census. Among the agricultural sectors, cultivation activity is registered in highest proportion with 82 per cent and agricultural labourers only 2 per cent. The population engaged in non-agricultural sector is considerably low with a proportion of 16 per cent. In valley area, the main workers engaged in cultivation activity are 47 per cent. However, the working population in non-agricultural activities is considerably high of 43 per cent. In Manipur, the two regions indicate wide disparity in workforce participation particularly in non-agricultural sectors.

Remarks

The process of urbanization is one desirable and essential for economic growth and social development. In other words, urbanisation has been an instrument of economic, social and political progress. The most striking immediate change accompanying urbanisation is the rapid change in the prevailing character of local livelihoods as agriculture or more traditional local services.

However, in Manipur, the concept of urban and its definition affect the statistics of urban population. For instance, de-classification of towns due to non-fulfilment of urban definition changes the figures. In the latest population census, only Moreh town is recorded as urban in the whole hill areas. In order to strengthen the urban system, the state needs a decentralised approach particularly emphasis to the growth of district headquarters. On the other hand, invest more economic infrastructure and administrative sharing rather than power centric in the Imphal capital.

What is need in the state is the real urbanisation process through adequate economic investment and social development. Today, the region manifests social and economic disparity between the hill areas and the valley areas. And this is considered a serious issue. Therefore, to narrow down the inter-regional disparities, there should be balanced economic and social development. Such balanced approach is necessary to bridge the economic differences and the most important is to bring social equality.

NOTE

1. Instruction Manual for filling up the Household Schedule issued by the Office of Registrar General and Census Commissioner, New Delhi, 2000.

REFERENCES

Amin, Samir. 1976. *Unequal Development: An Essay on the Social Formation of Peripheral Capitalism.* New Delhi: Oxford University Press.

Subba, Rao, B. 1958. *The Personality of India.* Baroda: MSU.

Suri, K.C., J.G. Bauer and J.R. Rele. 1988. *Analysis of Work Force in India.* Delhi:

Office of the Registrar-General and Census Commissioner, Controller of Publications.

Economic Survey Manipur, 2002-2004, *Directorate of Economics and Statistics.* Government of Manipur.

Statistics Handbook of Manipur, 2002, Directorate of Economics and Statistics. Government of Manipur.

3

Rural-Urban Migration in Assam: A Study in Relation to the Urban Informal Sector and Unemployment Levels

Dr. Nissar A. Barua & Dharmendra Nath

The process of development and modernization increases opportunities for mobility of people and thus creates conditions suitable for migration. Migration is the third basic factor after birth and death that affects the size of the population, besides altering the demographic character of the place of origin and the place of destination. More important is the fact that migration has an important bearing on the labour force, both in quantitative as well as in qualitative terms. Although international migration had hogged the limelight over the years, of late the focus has been on internal migration, and more so on *rural to urban* migration.

Migration is critical because it changes both the demographic and economic balance of groups within a given space. Hence, the "protection" of space and the economic opportunities that exist within it are often central objectives of the local population, while the expansion of opportunities within that space is a central objective of migrants (Myron Weiner 1978). The growing interest in the rural-urban migration flow has been due to the unparalleled movement of people from the rural countryside to the cities and towns of the developing countries, which are expanding at a tremendous rate. In fact the urban population in the developing countries had been estimated to grow from 275 million in 1950 to 1.45 billion in 1990, and then to over 2.1 billion in 2000 (UN 1980). This implies that the percentage of urban dwellers in the developing countries to the total urban population, had dramatically gone up from a mere 38% in 1950 to 60% in 1990, and then to 66% in 2000. Under these circumstances the rural to urban component of the flow is estimated to be highly significant, in terms of number, as well as in terms of their social and economic impact.

Internal migration has been classified in the Indian census operation as inter-state migration, inter-district migration and intra-district migration. Again the flow of migrants has been recorded as urban to urban flow, rural to urban flow, rural to rural flow, and urban to rural flow. From an economist's perspective the first two are relatively more significant since they have a huge bearing on the process of urban development, nature and size of its labour force, and the level of unemployment.

This paper will initially present the magnitude of internal migration that had taken place in Assam. The aim of this paper will be to explain the phenomenon of rural urban migration that had taken place and still continuing on a large scale. The largely unorganized informal sector in the urban areas of Assam is the principal employment provider to the people migrated due to economic factors. An attempt will be made to analyze the impact on the urban informal sector due to large scale migration from rural areas. The paper will also highlight the problems associated with expanding unorganized urban informal sector. The urban unemployment scenario in Assam is no better. Despite the presence of a large unemployed urban labour force, rural urban migration is continuing and thus fuelling the urban unemployment rate. An attempt will be made to explain urban unemployment in the light of the Todaro model. Finally, the impact of rural urban migration on urban development and unemployment will be highlighted and their bearings on policy prescription will be analyzed.

Migration in Assam: Magnitude and Types

Migration had always been an important and contentious issue in Assam. The number of migrants in relation to the total population was on the higher side in 1971-81, when it constituted 8% of the total population at 13.42 lakhs; this trend continued in 1981-91, when the number of migrants increased to 19.88 lakhs, comprising about 9% of the population.

In Assam, intra-district migration has dominated internal migration. However a distinct pattern is observed to indicate that the percentage share of this form of migration in the total migration had fallen from 65.31 % in 1971-81 to 63.15% in 1981-91. From the perspective of this paper a more significant stream of movement is constituted by inter-district migration whose volume had increased over the years from 3.24 lakh in 1971-81 to 5.47 lakh, in 1981-91. The increase in its percentage share in the total volume of migration in the same period, from 24.14% to 27.52%, has interesting implications in urban growth and the level of unemployment.

Table 3.1: Percentages of Migrants by Various Types in Assam (by Place of Last Residence)

Type of migrants	*1981-91*	*1971-81*
Intra-district	12,55,791	8,76,518
	(63.15%)	(65.31 %)
Inter-district	5,47,355	3,23,997
	(27.52%)	(24.14%)
Inter-state	1,66895	1,19,242
	(8.39%)	(8.88%)
International	18,387	22,416
	(0.92%)	(1.67%)
All types	19,88,428	13,42173

Source : Census of India, Migration Table, Assam, 1991, Vol. 1 (Table D-1)

Migrants from Bihar dominated inter-state migration into Assam. They were followed in substantially lower numbers, by migrants from West Bengal and Uttar Pradesh. Confining the movement within the northeast, there were significant number of migrants from Tripura and Meghalaya into Assam. However migrations from the other northeastern states were relatively less significant. Ignoring the popularly perceived large scale illegal migration from across Assam's international border, the total number of legal migrants, i.e., immigration during the 1981-91 was 18,387 which were smaller than the 1971-81 figure of 22,416. As expected the migrants in this category were mostly from Bangladesh (64.1%), followed by Nepal (18%). Among the immigrants of 1981-91, 64.8% have settled in rural areas whereas the rest have moved into urban areas.

Pattern of Migraiton Streams

The rural to rural stream dominates all migration streams at the three levels, i.e. inter-state, inter-district, and intra-district. However over the past two decades there has been a reduction in its share for all the above-mentioned levels. Thus, the share of rural to rural migration at the intradistrict level declined by almost 4 percentage points over the decade from 1971-81 to 1981-91 whereas the fall at the inter-district and inter-state level were 20 percentage and 3.1 percentage points respectively in the same period of time. In contrast, the share of rural to urban migration in the state has exhibited dramatic increase over the same decade. At the intradistrict level, its share had gone up from 5.4% to 8.2 %, whereas at the interdistrict level the gain has been from 10.9% to 20.1 %; an impressive 9.2 percentage points. In absolute terms, rural to urban migration had gone LIp from 47,012 to 1,03,447 at the intradistrict level over the decades from 1971-81 to 1981-91, whereas at the inter-district level it had increased from 35,171 to 1,10,004. The fact that the percentage share of this flow diminished at the inter-state level by 1% does go against the run of play. However it must be pointed out that the absolute number of migrants had gone up from 35,175 to 47,592. The impressive increase in the rural-urban flow within the expanding volume of internal migration raises some interesting questions. Is the growing urbanization of the state responsible? If so, are adequate numbers of employment opportunities created in the formal sector of the rapidly expanding towns and cities of the state to justify such a growing inflow or are there silent and unsung informal sectors to absorb the pressure of the flow? Finally the question must be raised why rural migrants stream into towns and cities despite the fact that the unemployment rate there is relatively high? On the other hand urban to urban migration in the intradistrict level is relatively small. Finally, the relatively modest growth in urban to rural migration has opened up a new line of argument.

Table 3.2: Streams of Migrants between 1981-91 and 1971-81

Intra-district	*1981-91*			*1971-81*		
	Male	*Female*	*Total*	*Male*	*Female*	*Total*
Rural to Rural	3,62,700 (83.8)	7,36,601 (90.1)	10,99,30 I (87.6)	2,29,342 (88.4)	5,71 ,419 (92.6)	8,00,761 (91.3)
Rural to Urban	51,250 (II. 7)	51,250 (6.4)	103,447 (8.2)	19.360 (7.5)	27,652 (4.5)	47,012 (5.4)
Urban to Rural	11,190 2.5)	14,170 (1.7)	25,360 (2.0)	4,990 (I. 9)	9,700 (1.6)	14,690 (1.7)
Urban to Urban	13,255 (3.0)	14,428 (1.8)	27,683 (2.2)	5,670 (2.2)	8,385 (1.3)	14,055 (1.6)
All	438395	8/7396	1255791	259362	6/7156	876518
Rural to Rural	1,24,853 (51.5)	2,00,855 (65.8)	3,25,708 (59.5)	97,488 (71.4)	1,58,644 (84.6)	2,56,132 (79.0)
Rural to Urban	62,223 (25.7)	47,781 (15.7)	1,10,004 (20.1)	22,713 (16.6)	12,458 (6.6)	35,171 (10.9)
Urban to Rural	14,028 (5.8)	16,350 (5.4)	30,378 (5.5)	3,514 (2.6)	3,900 (2.1)	7,414 (2.3)
Urban to Urban	41,213 (17.0)	40,052 (13.1)	81,265 (14.9)	12,805 (9.4)	12,475 (6.7)	25,280 (7.8)
All	242317	305038	547355	136520	187477	323997

(Contd.)

Table 3.2: *(Contd.)*

Intra-district	*1981-91*			*1971-81*		
	Male	*Female*	*Total*	*Male*	*Female*	*Total*
Rural to Rural	36,810 (38.6)	29,894 (41.8)	66,704 (40.0)	24,587 (38.6)	26.790 (48.2)	51,377 (43.1)
Rural to Urban	30,310 (31.8)	17,282 (24.2)	47,592 (28.5)	22,713 (35.7)	12,458 (22.4)	35,171 (29,5)
Urban to Rural	8,488 (8.9)	6,849 (9.6)	15,382 (9.2)	3,514 (5.5)	3,900 (7.0)	7,414 (6.2)
Urban to Urban	19,818 (20.7)	17,399 (24.4)	37,217 (22.3)	12,805 (20.2)	12,475 (22.4)	25,280 (21.2)
All Streams	95426	7146	16,6,895	63619	55623	119242

Source: Census of India, Migration Table, Assam, 1991, Vol. 1 (Table D-2).

Reasons for Migration

The migrants had cited reasons such as employment, business, education, marriage, movement of family, natural calamities etc. as the reasons behind their migration within and into Assam. As evident from Table-3.3, migration among males to seek employment is relatively low at 9.9% of the total migration for intra-district flow. However it gets more significant for larger distances, as evidenced by the higher percentage share of 22.3% and 24.3% in the cases of inter-district and inter-state flow respectively. However among females, marriage appears to be the dominant factor inducing migration for all the three flows and followed by the reason stated as 'family moved'.

Focusing the analysis at the inter district level, employment as a factor inducing migration among males in the rural to urban flow emerges as the most significant with a share of 42% in the total volume of migration. Such a similar significant share is seen only in the case of urban to urban flow at 41.8%, whereas for this segment - the rural to rural and urban to rural is relatively insignificant. This reinforces the argument that the ever-expanding volume of rural to urban migration is induced by more attractive urban employment opportunities that makes the rural migrant flock into towns and cities looking for work and a better life.

Table 3.3: Percentage of Migrant Population indicating the Reasons for Migration by Various types

Reasons for migration	*Intra-district flows*		*Inter-district flows*		*Intel'-state flows*	
	Male	*Female*	*Male*	*Female*	*Male*	*Female*
Employment	9.9	0.9	22.3	1.9	24.3	3.3
Business	4.1	0.3	7.5	0.4	26.7	1.7
Education	3.0	0.8	4.3	1.4	2.7	1.5
Family moved	42.1	13.2	33.1	20.8	23.1	29.9
Marriage	3.7	75.0	2.2	64.1	1.9	52.6
Natural cal.	11.7	2.4	11.3	3.4	1.3	0.8
Others	25.5	7.4	19.3	8.0	20.0	10.2

Source: Computed from Migration Tables, Assam, 1991, Vol. -1 Table D-3), census of India

Table 3.4: Reasons for Migration by the Streams of Inter-district Migration

Reasons of Migration	*Streams of Migration*							
	Rural to Rural		*Urban to Rural*		*Rural to Urban*		*Urban to Urban*	
	% of Male	*% of Female*	*%of male*	*% of female*	*% of male*	*% of female*	*% of male*	*% of female*
Employment	11.4	1.0	25.6	2.0	42.0	4.8	40.8	4.0
Business	4.1	0.3	11.2	0.6	13.2	0.7	13.0	0.6
Education	2.1	0.7	4.2	1.2	9.0	3.5	7.2	3.4
Family moved	40.7	18.6	33.9	24.5	17.9	25.9	23.1	27.9
Marriage	2.8	68.5	2.9	63.3	1.2	52.7	0.9	52.6
Natural Cal.	18.1	4.6	4.0	1.2	0.8	0.6	0.3	0.2
Others	20.8	6.3	18.2	7.2	15.9	11.8	14.7	11.3

Source: Census of India, Migration Tables, Assam, 1991, Vol. 1 (Table D.10)

Finally Table 3.4 indicates the principal factors behind migration into major towns and cities of Assam. In the case of Guwahati, 41.4% of the total male migrants from rural areas have cited 'employment' to be the primary reason in their decision for migration, whereas the percentage of migrants who moved into the city to do business stood at 5.9%. Thus, the vast majority of rural migrants, i.e. 48%, into Guwahati, came in looking for better economic opportunities. The urban to urban flow for males into Guwahati exhibits a similar trait, though their percentage share in the total migration is marginally less. In the case of females, employment has been cited as a reason for migration by only 5.9% migrants from rural area and only 5.5% migrants from urban area, whereas 40% of the same migrants from both rural and urban areas attributed their movement to marriage. The same conclusions can be drawn broadly for the major towns of Assam, like Jorhat, Dibrugarh, and Silchar.

The trends indicated by Table -3. 5, are in keeping with our hypothesis that most of the male migration to urban centres are usually in search of more rewarding work. In a city like Guwahati where the formal sector exhibits a conservative rate of growth and hence is only able to create a limited number of employment opportunities, it is the vibrant informal sector which provides sustenance to the vast hordes of migrants. Guwahati stands out as the city to where most of the rural to urban and urban to urban migration takes place. With the total number of migrants at 1,42,490 in the period 1981-91, it stands far ahead of other major towns in Assam, like Jorhat, Dibrugarh, and Silchar, as a destination for migration. That is but natural considering the size of Guwahati's economy and its dynamic informal sector and the massive but less vibrant formal sector. This is also evident when we consider that the Kamrup district (whose head quarter is in Guwahati) is the highest contributor to the state's GDP (Baruah 2003). To substantiate the argument further we illustrate in Table-6, the fact that the migration to urban areas are not evenly spread but concentrated in the major cities and towns of their respective districts. Thus 96% of the migrants to urban areas of Kamrup district are concentrated in Guwahati city itself. This can be largely ascribed

Table 3.5: Reasons for Migration to Cities and Towns

Reasons	*Guwahati*		*Jorhat*		*Dibrugarh*		*Silchar*	
	From Rural	*From Urban*	*From Rural*	*From Urban*	*From Rural*	*From urban*	*From Rural*	*From Urban*
Employment								
Male	19550	12480	1578	730	1650	1450	1058	591
	(41.4)	(38.0)	(33.70	(34.6)	(44.7)	(46.3)	(35.5)	(33.9)
Female	1963	1610	350	110	170	190	200	110
	(5.9)	(5.5)	(8.0)	(404)	(4.7)	(4.9)	(6.7)	(4.9)
Business								
Male	5444	3573	610	340	370	350	400	130
	(11.6)	(10.0)	(13.0)	(16.1)	(9.4)	(11.2)	(13.4)	(7.5)
Female	200	140	20	30	30	40	60	30
	(0.6)	(0.5)	(0.5)	(104)	(0.9)	(1.0)	(1.0)	(1.3
Education								
Male	4870	2930	1020	420	570	500	210	80
	(10.3)	(8.9)	(21.8)	(19.9)	(15.3)	(16.0)	(7.1)	(4.6)
Female	1590	1500	210	120	180	210	120	60
	(4.8)	(5.2)	(4.8)	(4.8)	(5.6)	(5.4)	(3.6)	(2.7)
Family moved								
Male	6590	6440	820	430	460	541	920	650
	(14.0)	(19.6)	(17.5)	(20.4)	(12.4)	(17.3)	(30.9)	(39.7)
Female	9410	8220	810	530	660	940	960	790
	(28.2)	(28.2)	(18.5)	(21.2)	(18.2)	(24.)	(28.6)	(35.4)
Marriage								
Male	200	300	130	30	30	10	70	20
	(0.5)	(0.9)	(2.8)	(1.4)	(0.8)	(0.3)	(2.4)	(1.1)
Female	13580	11447	2620	1500	2190	2230	1654	1162
	(40.8)	(39.3)	(60.0)	(60.1)	(I 1.3)	(57.3)	(49.3)	(52.1)
Natural Calamity								
Male	170	80	20	0	0	20	0	0
	(0.4)	(0.3)	(0.4)	(0.0)	(0)	(0.6)	(0)	(0)
Female	110	60	30	0	10	0	0	0
	(0.3)	(0.2)	(0.7)	(0.0)	(0.3)	(0)	(0)	(0)
Others								
Male	10250	7103	510	160	640	260	320	230
	(21.8)	(21.7)	(10.9)	(7.6)	(17.8)	(8.3)	(10.7)	(13.2)
Female	6460	6140	330	206	390	280	400	80
	(19.4)	(21.1)	(7.5)	(8.1)	(10.7)	(7.2)	(10.0)	(3.6)
All Categories								
Male	47154	32906	4688	2110	3720	3131	2978	1741
Female	33313	29117	4370	2496	3630	3890	3354	2232

Source: Census of India, Migration Tables, Assam, 1991,. Vol. I (Table-DIO)

to the fact that the other towns in the district had been unable to attract a significant share of the migrants due to the inadequate size of their economy, which provides limited work. Principal district towns, like Jorhat and Silchar, exhibit the same trends. However Dibrugarh is an exception in the sense that it attracts only 47% of the total migrants to the district. This can be easily explained by citing the growth of the smaller industrial towns like Moran, Namrup, Duliajan etc.

Table 3.6: Concentration of Inter-district Urban Migrants in Certain Towns as Percentage of Total Urban Migrants to the District

Name of town	*Inter-district migrants from rural and urban areas to major towns as percentage of total migrants to urban areas of the district from rural and urban areas respectively*		
	Rural to urban stream	*Urban to urban stream*	*Total urban stream*
Guwahati	95%	97%	96%
Jorhat	84%	71%	80%
Dibrugarh	47%	65%	55%
Silchar	96%	73%	875

Source: Computed from Migration Tables, Assam 1991, Vol.1, (Table D2), Census of India.

Rural-Urban Migration and the Informal Sector

There exists a dual labour market in the urban areas, with two types of jobs: those in the 'traditional', 'marginal', 'unorganized' or 'informal' sectors, employing low skilled manpower at low wages; as against the more 'modern', 'developed' 'organized' and 'formal' sectors that employ the skilled at higher wages (Myron Weiner, 1978). A distinction is made between a 'core' region, where centralized authority makes its appearance and industrial development becomes more advanced, and a 'peripheral' region that is less developed and is usually at the 'geographical extremities of the state', with the core region recruiting its low-skilled, low-wage labour from the peripheral region (Michael Hecter 1976).

The last five decades have witnessed unprecedented growth of the cities and towns of the third world countries. The rapid growth in this case was fuelled by a population, which was multiplying at an explosive rate. And with the falling of birth and death rates in the urban areas, rural-urban migration had assumed an even more significant role for such dramatic increase in urban population. An estimate had indicated that rural migrants constituted anywhere from 35% to 65% of the recorded urban population growth, whereas in the case of India the figure of 45% had been earmarked to account for a part of 3.8% annual urban population growth. (Newland 1980).

Table 3.7: Population and Its Proportion to Total Population in Selected Districts

District	*Urban population*		*Urban population as a % to total population*	
	1951	*1991*	*1951*	*1991*
Kamrup	48,32]	655,2]5	7.65	32.76
Jorhat	16,]64	133,032	3.6	15.27
Dibrugarh	37,99]	] 83,850	8.06	]7.6]
Silchar	34,059	] 19,224	6.29	9.8]
Assam	344,831	2,487,795	4.29	11.10

Source: Census of India, 1991

In keeping with the trend in the developing countries, Assam also experienced a process of rapid urbanization. This was evident in the census figures, where the urban population went up from 344,83 I in 1951 to 2,487,795 in 1991, thereby increasing the percentage of urban population to the total population from 4.29% to 11.10%. Within the state, the urbanization process was the strongest in Kamrup district, where the percentage of urban population to the total population went up from 7.65% in 1951 to 32.76% in 1991. The extraordinary rate of urbanization of Kamrup was fuelled by the explosive growth of its principal city, Guwahati, which accounted for 89.18% of the district's urban population. Guwahati with a population of 584,342 is a thriving metropolis which powers the growth of the state. Included in that population is 142,490 migrants, who constitute nearly a quarter of the total population. This is a testimony to the size and dynamism of the Guwahati economy that it had attracted such a large number of persons into the city and also provided sustenance for them.

Of the total migrant population in Guwahati, 80,062 were males; amongst them the number of male rural migrants who had come into the city in search of employment numbered 19,550 whereas 12,480 males migrated into the city from urban area for the same reason. Similarly the number of male rural and urban migrants who moved into the city for business purposes numbered 5444 and 3573 respectively. Has the city generated adequate employment opportunities to absorb 41,047 migrants? The economy of Guwahati is dualistic in nature, which is characterized by the presence of a modern organized formal sector and an unorganized informal sector. It is the informal sector producing a vast assortment of goods and services that is responsible for creating most of the opportunities for sustainable work. There are some factors which makes the informal sector vibrant. First, very small-scale units, which are either individually or family owned, constitute the informal sector. This makes the entry of such a unit into the economy easy. Secondly, these units use very simple technology, which is labour intensive making their operating cost very cheap. Thirdly, labour intensive technology is economical because, most of the workers in this sector are illiterate and unskilled rural migrants who offer their services at low wages. Besides, for those workers who are self-employed, they are able to provide their products at a price, which is a fraction of what it would have cost in the formal sector. Finally, the lack of organization and official recognition means that most of the units in the informal sector need not register themselves with the official authorities, which exempts them from the constraint of regulation. Non-intrusion of labour laws and other social security compulsions mean that work can be created without the additional burden and cost of providing the necessary social security measures. Employers are free to 'hire and fire', and self-employed can change what they produce without any hindrance. All these factors impart flexibility and adaptability to the informal sector, which enables it to survive and flourish. And this inherent dynamism allows the informal sector to absorb the rapid addition to the labour force in diverse activities, ranging from hawking to construction labour, and from working as mechanic to serving as domestic servant. In fact, a study had revealed that the informal sector provides work to 20% to 70% of the urban labour force in the developing countries, the average being 50% (Sethuraman, 1981). If this is also true for Guwahati, then the informal sector has a crucial role to play in giving sustenance to the rapidly multiplying urban workers, especially to the rural migrants, considering the small base of the urban formal sector, in terms of output and employment. These conclusions can be extended for the smaller towns of Assam, although the size of the informal sector, the growth in the labour force and the volume of rural migrants will be of a smaller magnitude.

Besides providing sustenance to a huge chunk of urban labour force, the informal sector also provides an impetus to growth for the urban formal sector, by generating surplus for investment. It also enhances the competitiveness of the output of the formal sector by supplying cheap inputs for its production units. And to top it all, the urban informal sector, has a benevolent impact on the rural sector, where it eases the pressure of surplus rural population, by inducing some of them to migrate to urban centres.

Rural-Urban Migration, Urban Unemployment and the Todaro Model

There was a time when rural-urban migration was considered to be a natural process where surplus rural labour was recruited to provide the essential labour for urban development. However the tremendous influx of rural migrants into urban centres has left the towns and cities grappling with massive problems of urban unemployment. It is unanimously agreed that economic factors predominate in rural-urban migration. As articulated by Todaro, " These include not only the standard *push* from subsistence agriculture and *pull* of relatively high urban wages, but also the potential *pushback* toward rural areas as a result of high urban unemployment" (Todaro, 1993). More rural migrants into towns and cities tend to increase abruptly and disproportionately the supply of job seekers relative to the urban population growth. But the additional labour force cannot be absorbed in the urban centres, because creating more jobs here is more difficult and costly then it is in rural areas. "Together this rapid supply increase and lagging demand growth tend to convert a short-run problem of manpower imbalances into a long-run situation of chronic and rising urban surplus labour." (Todaro, 1993)

Confining the discussion to Assam, the problem articulated in the earlier segment is vindicated when it is confronted with empirical data. Thus, of the 224 lakh population of Assam in 1991, 13.54 lakhs are urban male; among them 9.43 lakhs joined the labour force of which, 58,000 failed to get gainful employment. This implies that the unemployment rate among urban males stands at 6.15%. Similarly the unemployment rate among urban females stands at 28.72%. The huge differential between urban male and female unemployment rate falls substantially in the case of rural labour force; however it is still significant at 6.2% for rural males against 14.31 % for rural females. However in the context of rural-urban migration, the focus is on the differential between rural and urban unemployment rates; here the differential between female unemployment rates in rural and urban areas is very significant, though it has a little bearing in the volume of female rural- urban migration. This is simply because marriage or migration of the female's family determines the decision for migration, and not employment. However things are very different in the case of male rural-urban migration, where employment is considered to be the principal factor motivating the potential rural migrant. The rural unemployment rate in Assam (6.2%) is only marginally higher than that of the urban rate (6.15%), and as such cannot be a compelling reason for relocating to urban areas.

The Todaro model assumes that migration is essentially an economic phenomenon and the existing rural-urban income differential can adequately explain the rural-urban flow of migrants despite a high rate of urban employment. "The fundamental premise is that migrants consider the various labour market opportunities available to them in the rural and urban sectors and choose the one that maximizes their expected gains from migration" (Todaro 1993).

Table 3.8: Total Population, Economic Active Population, and Unemployed Population, Assam, 1991

Category	*Rural*		*Urban*		*Total*
	Male	*Female*	*Male*	*Female*	
Population	1030 4 (45.97)	9622 (42.93)	1354 (6.04)	1134 (5.06)	2241 4 (100)
Economically Active Population	7145 (65.36)	2662 (24.34)	943 (8.63)	181 (1.64)	1093 (100)
Number of Unemployed	443 (47.43)	381 (40.79)	58 (7.28)	52 (5.57)	934 (100)
Unemployment Rates	6.2%	14.3%	6.15%	28.73 %	

(a) The economically active population is estimated on the basis of the total population and the labour force participation rate of that population.

(b) The unemployed population is estimated on the basis of the economically active population and the unemployment rate.

(c) Figures in parentheses represent percentage of the total.

Source

I. Population in Assam by sex and rural-urban distribution: Socio-Cultural Tables, Census of India, 1991, Part-IV, A-C Series.

2. Labour Force Participation Rate: NSSO, 50th round.

3. Unemployment Rate for Assam: NSSO, 50th round

In full or near full employment economies of the developed countries, the decision for migration is a simple one; the rural workers migrate to take up higher paid urban job in the face of rural-urban wage differentials. However the economies of the developing countries are beset with substantial unemployment, especially in the urban sector. Under these circumstances a potential rural migrant will weigh the rural-urban income differential with the possibility that he may remain without work for a considerable period of time before he finds an urban employment; this he will do by comparing expected urban income in a particular time period to the rural income. If the expected urban income exceeds the rural income, the decision to migrate would certainly be rational despite the existence of urban unemployment. However if the converse is true, our prospective migrants would abort such a course of action. "Rather than equalizing urban and rural wage rates as would be the case in a competitive model, we see that rural-urban migration in our model acts an equilibrating force that equates rural and urban *expected* incomes." (Todaro 1993). Thus, despite the high level of unemployment, the ongoing rural migration to urban areas would continue because the decision for migration does not depend solely on the unemployment rate, rather it is also significantly influenced by the rural-urban wage differential.

Policy Implications in the Context of Todaro Model

The Todaro model highly simplifies the phenomenon of rural-urban migration by presenting it as an adjustment mechanism, by which the labourforce allocate itself between rural and urban markets. But such a hypothesis appears credible in the case of Assam, when the rural-urban migration of males over longer distances is considered. Given the rural-urban wage differentials, the existence of high urban unemployment rates will not shield the towns of Assam and also its cities like Guwahati, from future influx of increasing volume of rural migrants. This is true, especially when we consider the fact that large-scale migration of mostly rural male indirectly induces *associational* migration of females also, who move in with the primary male member of their family. Under the given circumstances the Todaro model does have some policy implications.

Earlier discussions focused on the important role of the informal sector in absorbing a substantial part of the surplus resident manpower and also migrant labour in the urban centres. The lower unemployment rate and the shorter waiting period in this sector attract an ever expanding stream of rural migrants; and providing work along with the minimum basic amenities for all the rural migrants is the way beyond the combined capacity of both the urban formal and informal sector. The fallout in this case is aggravated by urban unemployment, formation of urban slums without basic amenities, congested streets, rising crime statistics and other ills which accompany urban life. Such a worst case scenario can be avoided if due care is taken to regulate the growth of the informal sector; this would include steps like registering small scale individual and family enterprises, and providing various incentives for their growth, which in turn would pave the way for their regulation. Other measures like creation of a satellite township and provision of infrastructure in the work place would go a long way in minimizing the birth pangs that one associates with urbanization.

Another strategy prescribed to curb the proliferation of rural migrants in urban areas is to devise a special educational package designed to confine the rural population to the villages. However in developing countries, the demand for education is derived from the kind of job that a particular type or level of education promises. Hence there would be no takers for an education programme if it cannot guarantee a suitable job. On the other hand, the state's subsidized higher education induces the prospective rural migrants to undergo as many years of education as possible. This results in downward substitution in migration, where migrants with more years in school and college replace those with lesser number of years of education. This of course is a direct influence of downward substitution in urban employment, where labour with more formal education substitutes less educated worker, although the additional education remains largely unutilized.

Conclusion

In the light of the foregone discussion, it can be concluded that to have control over the urban unemployment level, one must be able to address the supply side of the rural-urban migration. The key to such a strategy is basically to minimize the rural-urban income differential, by adopting a comprehensive policy that would result in a sustained development of the rural sector. Such a policy must shed its urban bias to create non-existent social and economic infrastructures in the rural sectors, so that the rural income is sufficiently enhanced. Only this will motivate the prospective migrants, to refrain from moving into urban areas.

REFERENCES

1. Baruah, R.D., 2003, "Pattern of Migration in Assam during 1981-91 With Special Reference to Inter-District Migration." Paper presented in the 1CSSR sponsored national seminar on *Challenges of Development in the North East India.*

2. Directorate of Census Operations, 1998, *Socio-Cultural Tables, Census of India, 1991, Part IV, A-C Series.* Directorate of Census Operations, Assam.

3. Directorate of Census Operations, 1998, *Migration Tables,* Vol: 1, Census of India, 1991 Series-G, Assam. Directorate of Census Operations, Assam.

4. Hecter, Michael, 1976, "Ethnicity and Industrialization: On the Proliferation of the Cultural Division of Labor," *Ethnicity,* Vol. 3 (1976).

5. Newland, K. 1980, "City Limits: Emerging Constraints on Urban Growth." *Worldwatch Paper No.* 38, Washington DC.

6. Sethuraman, S.U. 1981, *The Urban Informal Sector in Developing Countries.* International Labour Organisation, Geneva.

7. Todaro, M.P. 1993, *Economic Development in the Third World.* Orient Longman Limited, Hyderabad (A.P.), India.

8. United Nations. 1980, "Pattern of urban and rural population growth," *Population Studies* 68.

9. Weiner, Myron, 1978, *Sons of the Soil- Migration and Ethnic Conflict in India,* Oxford University Press, Delhi.

4

Transportation as Tool to Streamline Urban Structure

M. Manas Singh

Introduction

It is a well known fact that growth of a settlement is greatly dependent on transportation. The most rudimentary form of physical connectivity is surface transport and through it movement of goods, people etc. from one place to another is made ultimately supporting the economy in many ways. Mention may also be made here that urban form and urban structure also shape the transportation characteristics of a city. In other words, urban structure and form and transportation are interrelated.

The spatial distribution of home, jobs and other activities are followed by a circulation system. A city that exhibits a harmony between supply and demand parameters is considered to be in 'stable state'. However, in the urban transport, demand and supply equation is not balanced and demand invariably outstrips supply. In Manipur, transportation system primarily consists of road network only.

Urban Form and Urban Structure

Urban form is the physical arrangement of various functions like residence, work places, commercial areas etc. On the other hand, urban structure is the way in which population, employment and other economic activities are distributed on the urban area.

Generally, cities/towns that have grown over a period of time are circular or radial in form. Being a city belonging to this category, the Imphal city is mono-centric and consequently the road network is also radial in pattern. Due to this, the Central Business District (CBD) comprising of Khwairamband Bazar and surrounding areas have developed as a strong core. Most of the economic and administrative activities continue to be located there. This has resulted in transportation system/network encouraging concentration of activities. Perhaps, Imphal is one of the very few small cities in the country where three National Highways (NH-39; NH-53; NH-150) meet right at the heart of the city. This ultimately results in the 'through traffic' i.e., those traffic having no business or purpose in the city to ply in the central area, thereby increasing the congestion level. Thus, Imphal city has almost reached a 'saturation point'.

Urbanization and Problems of Imphal

There has been a significant increase in urban population of Manipur during the past few decades. In 1981-91, the state's urbanization level was 27.52%, which is higher than the national average of 25.77%. In 2001, Manipur's urbanization level was at 23.88%. The decline in urbanization level from 1981-91 to 1991-2001 can be attributed to the fact that some towns in hill districts were denotified.

But the urban area lying in the valley districts has not commensurately increased, implying that the existing area was densified. Also, there is a greatly skewed distribution of urban population among the valley districts, Imphal (east and West) districts have maximum urban population of more than 63% of the total population of the state (3.50 lakhs out of 5.55 lakhs as per 2001 census). The remaining areas of Manipur depend heavily on Imphal for both economic and administrative reasons. This interaction, almost on a daily basis imparts a tremendous pressure on the CBD area of the city. The overall level of service of various infrastructures like transportation, water supply, sewage etc., had declined due to the day -to- day influx of persons from outlying areas of the state to central Imphal. Now the question is how to curb this trend and save the city from further deterioration?

Thus, we need to adopt a strategy whereby the economic and administrative activities from the central area is decentralized and existing urban area, properly streamlined. In short, the city needs to undergo 'restructuring'.

From a historical perspective, Imphal has already had peripheral activity centres in the form of markets like Singjamei, Khurai Lamlong , Kwakeithel etc. But presently, they are not very effective in weaning away economic activities from the CBD area. One important reason for this may be they are too near to the CBD area and have almost amalgamated with the city core with their identity obscured by the imposing characteristic of Khwairamband Bazar.

Hence, we have to develop activity centres (employment and business) at the periphery of greater Imphal or at towns other than Imphal, so that they may effectively act as a 'counter magnet' and draw away share of activities from Imphal city core. The need to adopt polynucleated development (where self-reliant activity centres are located away from the city centre) is of paramount importance now. The issue is 'how to achieve the desired objective and where should we locate the new activity centres?"

Transportation Related Interventions

As mentioned in earlier paragraphs, transportation and urban structure are interrelated. Thus, it can be effectively employed as a 'tool' to achieve the desired objectives of restructuring the urban form and structure. However, it is worth mentioning that transportation is not the only tool, but one among the most useful planning tools to restructure an urban structure/form. For achieving an optimal result, a well balanced urban structure-transportation system has to be brought out.

The transportation related interventions that can encourage restructuring the city:

1. The proposed activity centres must be located along the transportation corridors so that they are accessible to the public. This is because restructuring without consideration for transportation system will lead to an undesirable state, having lesser social utility.

2. The impedence level on making trips should be minimum. Higher the impedence level, lesser would be the propensity to make trips to/fro activity centres. Impedence may be in terms of cost, travel time, comfort level, frequency etc.

3. A good transportation system and logistics have to be adopted in order to ensure higher flow of 'people trips' to the activity centres. Some suggested measures may be – (i) encourage public transport operators to ply on these routes by giving 'incentives' in the form of reduced license fee, lesser taxes etc. (ii). Concessional fares for passengers, (iii) lesser parking fee at the new activity centres and (iv) better scheduling of public transport system. By doing so, the economic as well as administrative activity level will increase in these centres, thereby relieving the pressure from the city core.

4. Developing transportation corridors with good and reliable transportation system in outlying areas or sparsely populated zones of greater Imphal will effect higher population and employment density along these corridors due to the increased accessibility. Transportation can be used to change the density of population /employment, which is important component of urban structure.

5. The through traffic, having no purpose in CBD area of Imphal needs to be diverted by constructing bypass/ ring road. The master plan of Greater Imphal -2011 had envisaged ring roads on both western and eastern side of the city so as to bypass the through traffic from NH-39 and NH-53. These ring roads will also connect the major roads radiating from the central area to the National Highways.

6. The resulting circumferential pattern of road network will be instrumental in shifting the current urban form from a radial to circumferential one. This will reduce the stress on the central core area.

Conclusions

1. The urbanization level of Imphal city has almost reached a 'saturation level'.

   Further densification of the city or establishing new activity centre that can attract people from outlying areas should not be encouraged.

2. There is a need to change the predominant urban form from currently mono-centric with redial roads to polycentric one. Various components of urban structure are to be located accordingly.

3. There is a genuine need to set up alternative 'self reliant' actIvIty centres away from the city core so that the burden on the existing infrastructure of the city is reduced.

4. Those activity centres must be located at areas near and accessible to transportation network.

5. General public must be educated on the need to decentralize the city. The old habit of only Khwairamband bazar has to undergo a change.

6. Transportation can be employed to change population and employment densities.

   Thus, by adopting proper policy decisions, desired areas of Greater Imphal can be made to undergo controlled densification by introducing compatible transportation systems.

7. Public transport system should be streamlined by ensuring proper scheduling of buses, frequency, and identification of routes. The strengthening of mass transport system will help in reducing the dependence on private mode of transport or Intermittent Public Transports (IPTs).

5

Urban Development and Indigenous Peoples of Manipur

Jiten Yumnam

Rapid urbanization that varies across the globe brought many environment risks and problems and in almost unplanned cities and towns of developing countries the conflict between environmental resource base and developmental needs amidst urbanization is palpable. Increasing number of countries now recognize certain key principles of sustainable urban development, that respects environment as a resource to be carefully managed on sustainable basis incorporating the principles of precautionary approach with respect for carrying capacity of ecosystem and preservation of opportunities for future generations. Undeniably, the challenge of urban planning and management lies among others in the application of sustainable development principles as the impact of unsustainable urban development initiatives, land uses pattern and its impact on environment and human survival are well documented.

Degradation and loss of environment signify loss of the culture, tradition and the identity of indigenous peoples of Manipur, a small state brooding Nagaland, Assam, Mizoram and Myanmar bearing a profound spiritual and material relationship with their lands and resources in all social, cultural and political dimensions. Their folklores, rituals rejuvenating the rivers, hills, wetlands best exemplify this intrinsic relationship.

Any disrespect towards them invites perennial wrath and misfortune to indigenous peoples.

The expansion of towns and cities gives enormous pressure on natural resources such as lakes and rivers. Development in the state has been largely imposed with complete disregard for the right of indigenous peoples to participate in the decision-making, impeding them from proceeding with their own forms of development consistent with their own values, needs and perspectives. For instance, the Master Plan for Development of Greater Imphal, prepared in 1995 has been criticized for its failure to consult with the people, lack of adherence in its application and insensitive to unsustainable development principles. The concentration of extensive legal, political and economic power in the state has contributed to the problems of development. Much large-scale economic and industrial development has taken place in the state without recognition of and respect for indigenous peoples' rights to lands, territories and resources.

Countries in many parts of the world ignore the fact that communities, tribes or nations of indigenous peoples inhabit and use areas of land since time immemorial. Although the indigenous people concerned own the land and resources they occupy and use, countries disposes of the land and resources as if the indigenous people do not exist.

These government tendencies are further exacerbated in countries such as India, where state/provincial and even municipal government pursue such actions, either in coordination with the central or national government, or independently and in pursuit of their own policy. The Prime Minister of India, Dr. Manmohan Singh, in the presence of O. Ibobi Singh, Chief Minister of Manipur, laying the foundation stone for construction of Capitol complex at Kairang Khong, a wetland in Chingmeirong, in vicinity of Imphal, on 20 November 2004, presents a perfect synergy and coordination of central and state government in undermining the unique and intrinsic relationship of peoples of Chingmeirong, Thangmeiband and other surrounding areas with the Kairang Kong wetlands area. The disregard extends to the vital role that Kairang Khong wetland plays in the traditional water management of Imphal valley and the cultural and spiritual relationship with the Meitei people. It also worsens the water management and floods in Manipur.

The construction process of the Capitol Project of Imphal has been fraught with lack of transparency and an abject failure to consult with the indigenous peoples. The related detailed project report has not been disclosed to the people. Public hearing, a process of consultation with people was held arbitrarily only after the Kairang Khong wetland at Chingmeirong has been arbitrarily filled. The detailed Environment Impact Assessment (EIA), required under EIA notification of 1994 is still due. The arbitrary filling has already arbitrated the Amendment of 1st July 2004 to Environment Protection Act 1986 that requires any construction project falling under entry 31 (i.e. New construction projects) of schedules -I (of the EIA Notification) including new townships, commercial complexes, and office complexes for 1,000 (one thousand) persons or more with an investment of Rupees fifty crores or more, to obtain environmental clearance from the Ministry of Environment and Forests. No site clearance, no detailed EMP, no rehabilitation and Resettlement plan for the project exist till date.

Another dimension to the urban development and impact on indigenous peoples is the application of discriminatory legal doctrine where states have practically unlimited power to control or regulate the use of indigenous lands. The Manipur Land Registration and Land Reforms Act, enacted in 1960 to eradicate community land holding and establishing state's right over lands in Manipur empower states to take over land for various "public purposes". Section 4 of Land Acquisition Act, 1894 (Act 1 of 1894) applied while serving notice to residents of Chingmeirong, Thangmeiband, Lei Engkhol and other periphery locations at Kairang Khong for construction of Capitol Complex virtually means grinding poverty, displacement, homelessness and other misfortune for the indigenous peoples. The complicacy of legal recourse for compensation of land much undervalued will not be a viable recourse for people and will invite more hardships and undue inconveniences. And in fact, the compensation and rehabilitation history in Manipur presents a grim reality. A detailed rehabilitation policy is still absent in Manipur. The Mapithel Multipurpose Project affected villagers in Manipur continue to lament that the government fails till date to implement the agreement entered on 19/06/1993 with the affected village for payment of full compensation.

Amidst glaring reality of urban development related evictions in Manipur over recent years arbitrating existing norms of development and human rights principles, any similar treatment towards residents in periphery of Kairang Khong wetland at Chingmeirong, Lei Engkhol would amount to perpetrating absolute injustice towards the people. Peoples seriously considered and characterized population transfers and forced relocation as a very serious inhuman problem. These involuntary transfer and relocation meant the loss of traditional ways of life with devastating consequences for the social and economic welfare of the communities concerned.

The International Labour Organization, convention 169 on indigenous and tribal peoples shall have the right to decide their own priorities for the process of development as it affects their lives, beliefs, institutions and spiritual well-being and emphasize that they shall participate in the formulation, implementation and evaluation of plans and programmes for development that may affect them directly. The UN Commission on Human Rights unanimously adopted the resolution on Forced Evictions (1993/77) on 10 March 1993, which affirms that every woman, man and child has the right to a secure place to live in peace and dignity and also affirms that practice of force evictions constitutes a gross violation of human rights. The Habitat Agenda, constituting commitments of government at the Habitat II Conference, Istanbul, Turkey, 3-14 June 1995 also mentioned that government must refrain from forced evictions and must ensure that the law is enforced against its agents or third party who carry out forced evictions. India is obliged to these existing global commitments and integrating these existing minimum standards and requirements for peoples in all urban developmental initiatives can foster meaningful respect towards promoting justice and equality.

Broader set of issues, concepts and perspectives in accommodating indigenous peoples' rights to lands and development should be developed by states and the negotiations undertaken with respect and recognition of the fundamental rights of communities can contribute to ongoing and lasting political and legal relationships. Such an alternative may prove to be more constructive to government and peoples. The construction of capital complex as a notion of development would be meaningless if the ideas and concepts of development, wishes and aspiration of peoples around Chingmeirong, Thangmeiband, Lei Engkhol etc. are not respected and incorporated. The ultimate decision and the right to or not to use their land should rest with the community and that development should not be authorized from others.

Urban management requires an approach focused on environment and development and there is coordination across sectors and agencies. Planning for all development even at all levels needs more inclusive, representative and democratic and should respond to the emerging priorities resulting from environmental concerns with an 'ecological system approach' that compares a location's carrying capacity to the potential impact from types of development.

Participatory planning in urban development can be a crucial indicator of the extent of the democratization of the country. City and town planning should engage the people in vIsIoning exercise that can identify the full range of issues facing a city. Planning a town or city should provide an assessment of social, economic and environmental trends and advice on what choices to make in order to achieve multiple and sometimes conflicting goals.

Sustainability of human settlements should be prioritized in all urban development in promoting economic and social development, human health and education, conservation of biological diversity, maintenance of cultural diversity as well as air, water, forests, vegetation and soil qualities at standards sufficient to sustain human life and well being for future generation. Institutionalizing a participatory approach to sustainable human settlements, developments and management prioritized effective participation of all actors especially women, persons with disabilities and indigenous peoples. Integration of the commitments of the Istanbul Declaration and Habitat Agenda UN Habitat II Conference, 1996 for a sustainable urban development, including protection of fragile ecosystem and environmentally vulnerable areas from the negative impacts of human settlements, promotion of peoples participation in urban development, reversal of the economic, environmental, social consequences of unplanned urban development and protection of historical, cultural and natural heritage, flora, fauna, as appropriate for indigenous and tribal peoples can contribute in securing meaningful urban development.

6

Urbanization and Landscape Planning of Imphal City: Problems and Policy Implications

Konjengbam Meghachandra Singh

Urbanization and Landscape Studies

Urbanization is a very complex and multifaceted phenomenon and its definition is thus nowhere uniform or universal. As Rao and Tewari has put it, "The understanding of the process of urbanization and its planning, cannot be limited to anyone discipline of study or compressed into one concept or one process or one problem". The definition of urban areas also differs from one country to another. Carter gives a wide range of definitions of urban population as adopted in different countries. It ranges from a simple definition adopted in Gambia to a much detailed one adopted in the former Czechoslovakia. In Gambia the definition of urban population is "Banjul Only" thereby signifying the population of a particular settlement area. In the erstwhile Czechoslovakia, urban centres are defined as 1) Large towns, usually of 5000 or more inhabitants, having a density of more than 1000 persons per hectare of built-up area, three or more living quarters 2) at least 15 percent of the houses, piped water and a sewage system for the major part at the town, at least five physicians and a pharmacy, a nine year secondary school, a hotel with at least twenty beds, a network of trade and distributive services which serve more than one town, job opportunities for the surrounding area, the terminal of a system of busy times and not more than 10 percent of the total population active in agriculture; 3) small towns, usually of 2000 or more inhabitants, having a density of more than seventy-five persons per hectare of built-up area, three or more living quarters in at least 10 per cent of the houses, piped water and a sewage system or at least part of the town, at least two physicians and a pharmacy, other urban characteristics to a lesser degree and not more than 15 per cent of the total population active in agriculture ; 4) agglomerated communities which have the characteristics of small town in regard to size, population density, housing, water supply and sewage, and percentage of population active in agriculture, but which lack such town characteristics as educational facilities, cultural institutions, health services and trade and distributive services, because these facilities are supplied by a town in the vicinity.

In India, the census definition of a town remained more or less the same for the period 1901-1951. According to the 1901 census, a town is defined as (i) every municipality of whatever size, (ii) all the civil lines not included within municipal limits, (iii) every cantonment, (iv) every other continuous collection of houses, permanently habited by not less than 5000 persons, which the Provincial Superintendent may decide to treat as town for census purposes. A town in 1961 census was determined on the basis of a number of empirical tests, these were: (i) a density of not less than 1,000 persons per square meter; (ii) a population of 5000 person; (iii) three-fourths of the working population should be outside of agriculture; and (iv) the place should have, according to the Superintendent of the State, a few urban characteristics and amenities. The 1971 census followed a slightly modified definition which defines town as, (a) all places having a municipality, corporation, or cantonment or notified town area; or (b) any other place which satisfies all the following criteria: (i) a minimum population of 5000, (ii) at least 75 per cent of the male working population being non-agricultural, and (iii) a density of population of at least 400 persons per square kilometer (i.e., 1000 persons per square miles). This definition of town was used in subsequent years.

Urbanization, a demographic process, is "an increase in the proportion of the urban population (U) to the total population (T) over a period of time". This process has the following two elements: (i) The multiplication of points of concentration and (ii) The increase in the size of individual concentration". These two elements are the result of three processes: (i) Population growth i.e., settlements previously classified as rural are re-classified as urban, (ii) excess of births over deaths (natural increase); and (iii) movement of people from non-urban to the urban areas.

Urban centres of varying sizes function as a system in any spatial unit.

As Tewari, et al. stated that in its totality, a city is part of a regional system, which in its turn, is a part of a national urban system. Larger towns, specially the capital cities, not only serve the surrounding areas but also the whole -regional urban system. It is in this aspect that the study of the landscapes of town particularly those of capital cities are important as such studies enable the understanding of different functional units within the urban centres.

The study of the urban landscape, often known as urban morphology', has attracted the interest of scholars in a number of fields; most importantly geography, but also in architecture, planning and, to a lesser extent, history.' Urban landscape studies include the layout of the street, the texture of buildings and the distribution of functional units, among others.

Landscape of Imphal City

Though the first settlement in Manipur is stated to be on the top of Koubru Mountain in the northern part of the state, streams of migrants formed the seven principalities or clans who settled in different parts of the valley. Each of the seven clans was headed by a chieftain (King of Piba) and used to function like that of the city states of ancient Greek. Manikchand observed that the seven principalities were closely knitted and allied ones, once settled in different parts of Manipur, each independent of each other. Imphal came under the most dominant principality, the Ningthouja, which made its capital at 'Kangla'. 'Kangla' was a walled area built for the ruling class and the common people lived outside the walled area. Later the settlement area expanded further and when the British came, the whole of Imphal was considered as urban. Though Imphal remained to be the only town till the 1961 census, its population decreased remarkably to 2,862 persons in 1951 as much of the area outside the walled area was declassified as new criteria of town was introduced with the coming of the Five Year Plans. However, again in the 1961 Census, with the expansion of the urban area, the urban population rose to 67,717 persons. Imphal's urban population was 1000,366 in 1971,156, 622 in 1981, 2002,831 in 1991 and 228,419 persons in 2001.

Imphal town is roughly circular in shape. (Fig.l). The town is, however, elongated in the North and the South along the National Highway and the State Highway and in the west, the lowland area of Lamphelpat has been incorporated in the city. The layout of the city is radial pattern with streets radiating from the central part of the town in all directions. The two National Highways (NH 39 and NH 53), four State Highways viz., The Tiddim Road, the Ukhrul Road, The Yairipok Road and the Mayang Imphal Road and many other district roads radiate from the central part of the town.

Important administrative and commercial activities are concentrated in the central part of the city, in the west and south of the 'Kangla'. This area includes the main bazar, the Assembly Hall, the Raj Bhawan, Army Headquarters, the General Post Office, the Secretariat, the Chief Minister's Banglow, the Police Headquarters and other important government offices. Residential areas are located around this functional area. The Residential areas have houses of all classes and there are small market areas, educational institutions and other public uses and major functions. New government offices and other establishments are located in the northern and western part-of the city. The Northern part has a T.B. Hospital, an Office of the Agriculture Department, the office of the State Road Transport, storehouses and other industrial establishments. In the western part of the city, many government offices, which were previously

LEGEND

River............. ~

Road............. =

Site for new contruction... ////

Kilometers

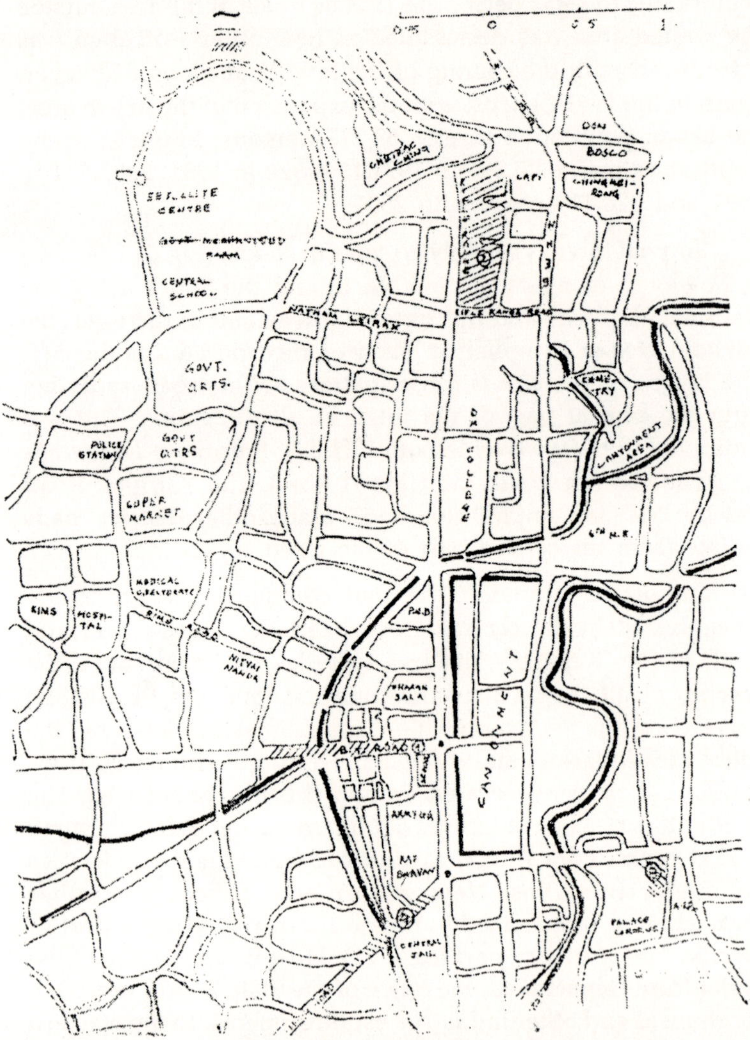

Fig. 1: Imphal City: Sites for new Constructions

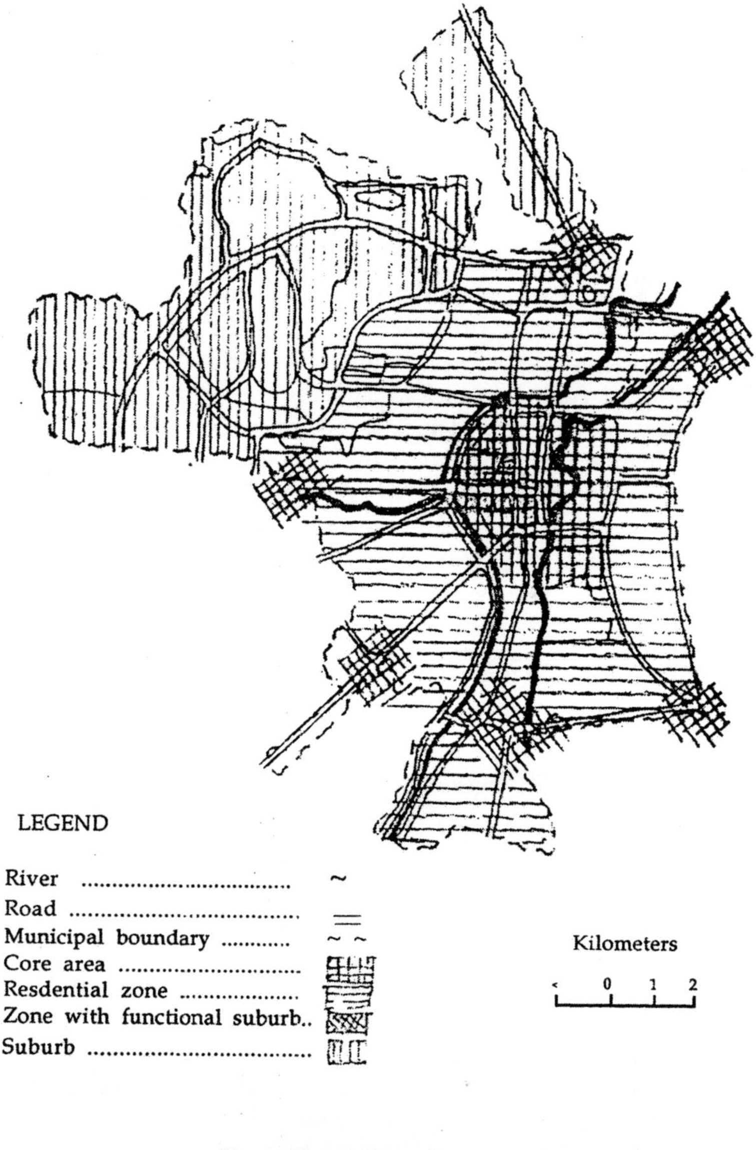

Fig. 2: Morphology of Imphal City

located in the central part of the town have been shifted. The area has the Central Agricultural University, the Zoological Garden, the Government Mechanised Farm and various government departments of the newly carved out Imphal West District. In the eastern part of the city, swamps and other wastelands have been reclaimed for the construction of building for housing a number of government officers for Imphal East District.

Four functional zones can be identified in Imphal City: (i) The Core area, (ii) The residential area around the core, (iii) The residential suburb with functional nuclei and (iv) the suburb (Fig. 1). The core area has administrative, economic, cultural and historical functions and attributes. The central core area comprises of the 'Kangla'. The palace compound and Govindajee Temple in the South of the 'Kangla' is an area of historical importance. The areas lying in the west and south of the' Kangla' form the zone of administrative economic functions and cultural activities. The market area in the west of the 'Kangla' has two distinct features - the women's market and the modern bazaar that extends over a large area.

The residential zone has developed around the city centre forming concentric zone. Houses built of bamboo and mud, mostly metal roofed, and modern 'pucca' houses (brick and RCC houses) are common. Schools and a few small open spaces are found in this zone. At major junctions of streets and roads small markets have developed.

The third zone includes residential areas with functional nuclei. They are beyond the residential zone at the outskirts of the city. The functional nuclei in this zone include the Kwakeithel Bazar, the Singjamei Bazar and Kongba Bazar in the southern part of the city; Lamlong Bazar and Sangakpham Bazar in the north and Naoremthong Bazar and Tera Bazar in the west. All these are located along the important transport lines. The fourth zone is the suburb of the town where few residential houses are found and new government establishment are built. The suburb includes the Lamphelpat area in the west and the Mantripukhri in the north along the National Highway (NH).

Population Pressure and Civic Amenities

The population of Imphal City has increased at a great pace during the last few decades. From 10,00,366 persons in 1971, it has been increased to 2,02,839 persons in 1991. In other words, the population of Imphal city was doubled in less than two decades. Here we can refer to some the basic civic amenities available in the city as recorded in the 1991 census (The table on housed and household amenities for 2001 is yet to be published by the census).

Table 6.1: Households and Distribution of Population by Availability of Electricity and Toilet Facilities

State/city	*Total number of households*	*Total population (per 1000)*	*Electricity availability to~ Toilet facility availability to*	
			Numer of house-holds	*Population I 'Number Population (per 1000) – ~ of households I (per 1000)*
	1	2	3	4c– 6–
Manipur	3,05,221	1.000	1,55,411	5131,31.646
Imphal	32,081	1,000	29,572	928 28,239 '- 89C

Out of the total number of 32,081 households in Imphal (U.A.) only 29,572 households were availed of electricity and 28,239 households were availed of toilet facilities (Table 6.1.). In other words, 2509 households, (72 persons per 1000) are without electrification facilities and 3842 households (104 persons per 1000) are either sharing toilets with others or using public facilities. And out of the total number of 32081 households only 22,436 households are availed of tap water and the rest 9645 households are depending on wells, handpumpsl tubewells, river! canal and other sources (Table 6.2). Imphal city also lacks a comprehensive sewerage system.

Table 6.2: Households Classified by Source of Drinking Water, Availability of Electricity and Toilet Facility in Imphal (D.A.)

Source of drinking water		I Total number - of households	Electricity: Available		Not available	
			~ Toilet			
			Available	Not available	Available	Not available
I		2	3	4	5	6
All sources	Total	32,081	26,612	2,960	1,627	88?
	within premises	13,561	12,170	933	370	88
	Outside premises	18,520	14,442	2,027	1,157	794 ~
Well	Total	1,436	1,122	210	71	
	Within premises	968	792	115	41	20 I
	Outside premises	468	330	95	30	13 I
Tap	Total	22,436	19,095	1,861	974	
	Within premises	10,607	9,619	720t	218	y ~
	Outside premises	11,829	9,476	1,142	7-c 6~	=13i~
Handpump/ tubewell	Total	1,459	1,084	246 ;	63	66,_
	Within premises	116	98	I	3	- 6 I
	Outside premises	1,343 I	986	237 i	60	60 v
River/canal	Total	719	351	150 i	61	Is7 ~
	Within premises	42	38	1	2 1	1 I
	Outside premises	677	313	149 ~	59 ~	1s6 ~
Tank	Total	3,348 I	2,643 1	304	346 j	
	Within premises	1,428	1,256 1	101i		

	I	*2*	*3*	*4*	*5*	*6*
	Outside premises	1,920	1,384	2'I ; i i	245	S~I
Others	Total	2,683 I	y?,317 I	FS	112	06
	Within premises	400	364	27 ' S ! I'		
	Outside premises	-I		i		

Landscape Planning and Policy Implications

Landscape planning of Imphal City can be seen in the context of (i) the rapid population growth of Imphal city, (ii) the existing infrastructure and other civic amenities, (iii) the project being taken up at present and (iv) Policy Implications. Imphal, the capital city of Manipur, is witnessing a decadal population growth rate of above 25 percent during the recent decades. And as mentioned above, the city's population was doubled in a short span of two decades from 1971 to 1991. It has also been mentioned that the city is facing acute shortages of even basic civic amenities like drinking water, electricity and toilet facility. The city also lacks adequate number of parks, walking tracks, and open spaces. There is a poor drainage system and almost every street and even the houses are inundated during torrential downpours. And due to lack of sewerage systems, every household is compelled to spend thousands of Rupees on toilets.

It is in this context that some of the important projects taken up by the government can be critically examined. In this paper I propose to take up four such projects; viz., i) The Flyovers, ii) The Capitol Projects, iii) The Cultural Complex, and iv) The Imphal Sewerage Project.

i) *The Flyovers*: Though the objective of the construction of flyovers is to reduce or remove the burden of traffic congestion, the location of the flyovers in the city will not serve the purpose. The B.T. Road Flyover, the construction of which has already been started, is located in the small, rare and historically symbolic space in the heart of the city. The diverted traffic will descend, in the east, in front of a theatre, a school, offices and commercial complex. A road would also converge from the south coming from the Governor's road via the State Museum. As soon as the traffic descends the road meets the right angled T-junction at the western gate of the Kangla. And the flyover is not needed at all in the heart of the city. Similar is the case with the one proposed to be constructed on the Keishampat bridge. The flyover, running over the bridge will descend near the main gate of the Governor's Palace thereby disturbing the skyscape of the palace. At the same time it will also pose a security concern to the Palace as the flyover will run close to the boundary wall of the Palace.

ii) *The Capitol Project*: Even before Prime Minister Manmohan Singh laid the foundation stone of the project, on 20th November, 2004 concerted effort was made by individuals and organizations to save the culturally symbolic rare open space. And the government did not make a clear cut agenda on the project. There was a perception of mass eviction of land for the project from the rightful landowners and settlers". Thus, the government finally gave in to the public pressure and announced that the Project would house only the Assembly Hall and the High Court and Secretariat would be moved to Mantripukhri. The Cultural Complex at Palace ground also displayed similar lack of planning and vision.

The French assisted Imphal Sewerage Project has two components – sewerage network system and sewerage treatment plant. However this project is also at stake as the Government is pursuing at a slow pace. The cost of the project is ever increasing as additional money is to be paid to Calcutta dockyard for holding the equipments and as the prices rise with time.

Landscape planning in the city should address the issue of open space and rational utilization of space by addressing people's sentiments. Measures should be taken to decentralize the development projects to the periphery to prevent congestion in the city centre.

REFERENCES

I. V.L.S. Prakasa and Tiwari (1978), *The Structure of an Indian Metropolis: A Study of Bangalore,* New Delhi: Allied Publishers Private Limited.

4. Tewari, et.al. (1986), *Indian Cities: Ecological Studies.* New Delhi: Concept Publishing Company.

5. Whitehand and Larkham (ed.), *Urban Landscape: An International* Perspective

6. Laiba, M.T. (1992), *The Geography of Manipur,* Imphal.

7. Manikchand, Konsam(1988), The Evolution of the Meitei State, in Sanajaoba(ed.), *Manipur Past and Present.* Vol. I, New Delhi.

8. Singh, Konjengbam Meghachandra(1999), *Structure of Urbanization of the Frontier Eastern State: A Case Study of Manipur.* Unpublished M. Phil dissertation. Chandigarh, Geography Department, Panjab University.

9. Singh, Konjengbam Meghachandra, *The Sangai Express,* April 29, 2005.

10. Singh, Konjengbam Meghachandra, *The Sangai Express,* Dec. 28, 2004.

11. *The Sangai Express,* April 21, 2005.

12. *The Sangai Express,* April 21, 2005.

13. Census of India. Primary Census Abstract, 2001.

14. Census of India. Series 15. Manipur. Part VI1. Tables on Households and Household Amenities.

7

Urbanization, Urban Livelihood and Access of Basic Urban Services in North-East India

Kalyan Das

Introduction

The Census of India, 2001 data revealed that just about 15 percent people of northeast India live in urban areas. This figure for tne country as a whole was 27.7 percent. The region though constitutes a smaller proportion of urban people as compared to the country as a whole at present northeast India is showing a more vibrant pace of urbanization. Most of the states in the region namely Assam (36.2 percent growth during 1991-2001), Meghalaya (37.1 percent) and Mizoram (38.7 percent) have maintained a pace above the national rate of 31.1 percent growth of urban population. On the other hand the pace of urbanisation is much higher in the states of Nagaland (69.4 percent) and Arunachal Pradesh (101.3 percent). Manipur (12.8 percent growth) in other extreme showed a very slow pace along with Tripura (28.8 percent) in the growth of urban population (Table 7.1). Number of towns in the region on the other hand has increased from 195 in 1991 to 244 in 2001.

What are the reasons for relatively higher growth of population in urban areas of the northeastern states in the 1990s? Data of Sample Registration System (SRS) reflects that

Table 7.1: Growth of Urban Population in North Eastern States of India

States	*1981*	*1991*	*2001*	*Growth 1981-91*	*Growth 1991-2001*
Arunachal	41428	110628	222688	167.04	101.29
Assam	-	2487795	3389413	-	36.24
Manipur	375460	505645	570410	34.67	12.81
Meghalaya	241333	330047	452612	36.76	37.14
Mizoram	121814	317946	441040	161.01	38.72
Nagaland	120234	208223	352821	73.18	69.44
Tripura	225568	421721	543094	86.96	28.78
India	159727357	217611012	285354954	36.24	31.13

Source: Census of India, Various Years

the region shows much lower natural growth rates in urban areas over the past three decades compared to the country as a whole (Table 7.2). This leaves to explore the other cause of rise of population that is movement of people from rural areas both from within the states as well as from other states to the urban areas of the region. To capture information on this aspect the migration data for the 2001 census is still not available. However, the available data from 1991 census provide us some insight. The 1991 census data on migration reflect that out of the total migrants, inclusive of intra-state, inter-state and international more than half of them (54.3 percent) had moved into the urban areas of the state of Arunachal. This is to the reference period of past 0-9 years. These proportion of migrants moved to the urban areas of the other states in the region were 45.7 percent in case of Mizoram, 40.9 percent in Nagaland, 33.9 percent in Meghalaya, 21.2 percent in Manipur, 16.3 percent in Tripura and 15.3 percent in Assam (Table 7.3). Considering the level of urbanization in the states of the region these proportions of migrants explain the rapid urbanization process in the region. The Table also reflects that intra-state rural to urban movement constitutes the larger share of migrants in all the states.

Table 7.2: Natural Growth Rate of Population in Urban areas of North Eastern States

State	*1971*	*1981*	*1991*	*1997*
Arunachal	-	19.8 in 1982	20.5	10.2
Assam	21.5	15.2	14.4	14.8
Manipur	20.9	19.9	12.3	11.4
Meghalava	-	14.2	14.7	12.2
Mizoram	-	NA	NA	NA
Nagaland	-	17.2 in 1983	9.3	5.2
Tripura	15.5	9.4	9.1	9.7
India	20.4	21.4	17.2	15.0

* *Source:* Compendium of India's Fertility and Mortality Indicators, RGI, New Delhi, 1999

Table 7.3: Proportion of Migrants in Urban Areas of the States of North Eastern States, 1991 Reference Period-0-9 Years

State	*Total migrant in 1991*	*Intra-state Rural-urban*	*Inter-state Rural urban*	*Inter-state urban urban urban*	*Inter-national to urban areas urban*	*Share of migrant migrant in urban*	*Percen-tage of urban popula-tion in 1991*
Arunachal	180559	43.1	6.5	4.3	0.4	54.3	12.8
Assam	200398 1	10.7	2.4	1.9	0.3	15.3	1 1.1
Manipur	35374	14.4	3.6	2.9	0.3	21.2	27.5
Meghalaya	100557	15.7	8.7	8.0	1.5	33.9	18.6
Mizoram	49924	32.8	3.7	5.1	4.1	45.7	46.1
Nagaland	69375	19.7	11.4	8.4	1.4	40.9	17.2
Tripura	269474	10.6	0.9	1.7	3.1	16.3	15.3

* *Source:* Census of India, Migration Table, 1991

What are the reasons for movement of people from rural areas to urban areas? Employment, education, marriage, movement of family, natural calamities and quest for a safer space could be the main reasons for movement to the urban areas. The 1991 data reflected that majority of the people from rural areas inside the respective states of the region moved to urban areas of their states for seeking employment and livelihood opportunities. The proportion of these people were 40.2 percent in Assam, 48.9 percent in Manipur, 36.1 percent in Meghalaya, 31.5 percent in Mizoram, 61.7 percent in Nagaland, 27.4 percent in Tripura and 7.3 percent in Arunachal. Slow urbanization process in Tripura to an extent could explain the lower proportion of people moving to its urban areas for economic reason. However, the rapid urbanization process of Arunachal is externally induced than intra-state rural to urban movement of people. In urban Arunachal more than 60 percent migrant population are inter-state migrants moved in for various administrative, construction and trading activities. Overall figures are reflective enough that constraint in livelihood opportunities in rural areas of the region is one of the major causes of rapid urbanization in the region.

Is Rural North East India Really Plagued by Livelihood Crisis?

The whole region of north east India is relatively thinly populated (151 person per square km in 2001) compared to the country (312) as a whole and considered as resource rich. The proportion of people living below the poverty line in the states of the region, except in Assam is much less than the national average and showing a declining trend. On the other hand rural unemployment rate is also declining from whatever indication we get from National Sample Survey Organization (NSSO) data. These somewhat better pictures reflected during the reference period of NSSO 50th and 55th round (1993-94 to 1999-2000) do not in actual sense provide us the reality of livelihood crisis in rural areas of the region. Poverty ratio is declining in the region, but it is not that poverty is abolished in rural areas in north-east India. In rural areas of Arunachal (22.4 percent), Assam (40.2 percent), Manipur (14.1 percent) and Tripura (16.7 percent) still a significant section of people are living under poverty

(Table 7.4). It can be mentioned that the yardstick for measuring poverty in rural areas, that is income Rs. *3601* per capita per month is considered as grossly inadequate at present. In this context we avoid entering into the debate of poverty estimation in the country. On the other hand the figures of rural unemployment mismatch with the poverty ratio of the region. This means that the number of working poor outnumbers the number of people who are poor for want of work in rural areas of north eastern region. This means that the wages received by the workers is low and the number of days they are employed in a year is less in rural areas indicating inadequacy of work in rural areas (Kannan, 2005). On the other hand the percentage of households without cultivable land is increasing in most of the states of northeast India and this situation/of landlessness is becoming grave in the states of Assam and Tripura (Table 7.5). The region has also shown marginalization of workforce as well as rise of agriculture labourers in rural areas during the period 1991-2001. Market dependency of a large section of households for food grains also reflects constrains in livelihood in the region where more than 70 percent of population dependent on agriculture. At the same time unused cultivable land reflects institutional constraints for optimal utilization of the resources.

Table 7.4: Indicators of Livelihood Crisis in Rural Areas of North East India

State	*Rural poverty*		*Rural unemployment*		*Ruralmarginal workers*		*Agriculture labour*	
	1993-94	*1999-2000*	*1993-94*	*1999-2000*	*1991*	*2001*	*1991*	*2001*
Arunachal	41.5	22.4	0.8	0.2	1.0	6.3	5.1	4.5
Assam	45.1	40.2	7.3	1.9	4.9	9.3	12.1	18.2
Manipur	18.9	14.1	1.7	0.8	3.6	13.1	6.7	16.0
Meghalaya	24.3	6.0	0.2	0.2	2.4	9.3	12.5	23.3
Mizoram	6.2	2.9	1.4	0.7	6.8	1 1.5	3.0	7.6
Nagaland	2.3	0.2	1.7	1.3	0.4	7.1	1.4	4.8
Tripura	23.6	16.7	2.6	0.4	2.0	7.9	23.4	30.7
India			1.8	0.7				

* *Source*: NSSO 50th roudns and Census of India, 1991 and 2001.

Table 7.5: Indicators of livelihood Crisis in Rural Areas of North East India

State	*Percentage of households without cultivable land*		*Percentage of unused cultivable land*	*Market dependency of food grain of households*
	1993-94	*1999-2000*		*1993-94*
Arunachal	22.8	25.4	36.9	54.2
Assam	34.6	35.6	20.8	44.8
Manipur	24.7	16.2	14.6	36.4
Meghalaya	17.9	12.4	79.8	58.2
Mizoram	10.3	14.4	75.6	57.5
Nagaland	6.4	10.5	57.8	16.1
Tripura	54.0	57.9	9.1	70.5
India			26.7	59.7

* *Source* : Nedfi quarterly databank, January, 2003 and NSSO 50th round.

All these are enough to reflect the crisis of livelihood in rural areas of north eastern region and force people to move to urban areas in search of better livelihood. We can consider this as a push requiring to relocate surplus rural labour in urban space. Again the questions arise - are the urban areas capable of accommodating the exodus from rural areas? Are there enough jobs to accommodate them?

The Status of Urban Labour Market in North East-India

The data on rural unemployment of the region as well as for the country reveal that the pressure for jobs is more in the urban labour market. The urban unemployment rate on the other hand for the country and as well as for the region is higher than the rural unemployment rate. Rural unemployment rate is though relatively lower than the urban unemployment rate, the size of unemployed in absolute numbers is much higher in rural areas putting pressure in urban labour market as we have seen the movement of people from rural to urban areas for seeking employment and livelihood opportunities.

A look at the economic sectors of the country reveals that workers of some sectors are more concentrated in urban areas. It is argued that some activities are better performed in smaller space and require a density of population to be economically viable. Activities like financial services, transportation, trade and commerce are more concentrated in areas where there is more density of population or they can cover more people in minimum space. On the other hand activities like manufacturing and services can equally favour or be compelled to base their activities in urban as well as in rural areas of a country. Though the proportion of workers in these sectors to the total workers in a particular space set the criteria to define an urban space, these predominantly urban based sectors may not dominate the whole labour market in the north eastern region considering the fact that in this region 85 percent of population live in rural areas. Still it may be useful to see in what direction the urban job sectors of the region is moving in the recent past, particularly after the initiation of liberalization and opening up of the economy.

The urban centres of the north eastern region grew mainly to facilitate trade and services. The manufacturing base of this region is low and at present there is not a major livelihood generating sector. Manufacturing activities in no states of the region (except in Assam 8.3 percent in the organised manufacturing and in Manipur 10.3 percent in the unorganized manufacturing) contribute more than 2 percent to the state NSDP. Overall the economy of the region is moving more towards the urban based tertiary activities. It was seen that in Meghalaya (54.0 percent), Mizoram (59.2 percent), Nagaland (56.3 percent) and Tripura (55.2 percent) tertiary sector accounted for more than 50 percent of the NSDP in 1999-2000. In Arunachal (42.8 percent) and Assam (40.3 percent) the contribution of tertiary sector to NSDP has shown increases during the period 1993-94 to 1999-2000, whereas in Manipur it has shown a decline (41.6 percent). Though service sector (public administration, education) constitutes larger proportion of urban workforce (32 percent in Mizoram to 70 percent in Nagaland) it shows decline except in Nagaland and in Tripura (Tables 7.6a and 7.6b). The nineties show emergence

Table 7.6a: Usually Working Persons in Principal Status by Broad Industry Division -Urban Male

States		*Agri etc.*	*Mining*	*Manufacturing*	*Basic services*	*Construction*	*Trade, hotel, restaurant*	*Transport Services*	*Financial*	*Public administration Education commercial*
Arunachal	1993-1994	6.5	0	14.1	3.9	9.7	16.7	6.2	3.1	39.6
	1999-2000	6.4	0	0.5	2.2	12.9	33.3	1.2	1.0	42.4
Assam	1993-1994	2.7	6.6	9.4	0.7	3.1	32.5	8.9	2.1	34.0
	1999-2000	4.9	0.6	7.6	0.7	6.2	33.8	9.4	6.6	30.1
Manipur	1993-1994	30.0	0	4.2	1.7	3.9	11.0	4.7	2.1	42.3
	1999-2000	29.4	1.4	5.2	0	6.2	16.0	4.1	1.5	36.2
Meghalaya	1993-1994	2.4	0.2	1.9	0.6	9.2	21.9	2.0	2.2	59.1
	1999-2000	1.5	a	3.7	0.4	15.5	20.8	6.9	0.7	50.5
Mizoram	1993-1994	35.6	0.1	4.7	0.3	6.6	10.4	1.9	0.1	40.2
	1999-2000	23.8	1.8	4.3	a	1 1.9	14.2	4.3	2.5	37.2
Nagaland	1993-1994	4.5	0.6	4.9	0.3	8.3	25.2	4.4	2.1	49.8
	1999-2000	6.7	0	5.0	1.0	7.0	10.9	0.5	1.9	67.1
Tripura	1993-1994	5.6	0.7	9.0	0.4	2.6	21.2	7.5	4.2	48.3
	1999-2000	2.7	0	3.7	2	4.3	26.0	5.2	3.0	55.0
India	1993-1994	8.7	1.3	23.6	1.2	7.0	21.9	9.8	3.8	22.6
	1999-2000	6.5	0.9	22.5	0.8	8.8	29.3	10.4	4.4	16.5

* *Source:* NSSO 50th rounds.

of trading and banking, financial and real estate services as major contributor to NSDP and job opportunities in urban areas of the north eastern region. Trade activities including hotel and restaurants show a rising trend in all states except in Nagaland and Meghalaya. Except in Nagaland construction activities show a boom in urban areas of the region. The financial services sector in urban areas of north-east is yet to pick up except to some extent in Assam. It may be noted that many financial institutions have started their operations in banking and insurance sector in recent times stepping their foot in the gateway city of Guwahati. Considering the resource base of the region opportunities in the manufacturing industries leading to growth of construction, trade and financial services sector would have provided a vibrant and sustainable urban growth and livelihood opportunities in this region. The trend however is more towards residential construction and private transport boom and the towns are offering opportunities more in trade and hotel and restaurants and mostly in unorganized sector. The tertiarisation of the economic sector in this region is not based on a vibrant industrialization process or on an agriculture base.

From the earlier paragraphs we got an overall scenario of the urban jobs sectors in the region. However in recent times urban areas of the country see emergence of a labour market in the unorganized service sector and it is well anticipated in a poor development context. It is revealed from the NSSO data that the restaurant sector is one of the major sources of livelihood in the unorganized service sector in urban areas of north east India (Table 7.7). The proportion of people in the petty tea stall and restaurants in this region is more than the country average. Apart from this mechanized transport and transport related activities are another major source of urban livelihood in this sector. These jobs require virtually no skill and education constitutes 45 to 60 percent jobs in the unorganized service sector in urban areas of the states in the region. On the other hand education related activities are emerging as major livelihood provider in unorganized service sector in urban areas in the states of Assam, Manipur, Mizoram and Nagaland (Table 7.7).

Table 7.6b: Usually Working Persons in principal status by board industry division- Urban Female

States		*Agri etc.*	*Mining*	*Manufa-cturing*	*Basic services*	*Constru-ction*	*Trade, hotel, restaurant*	*Trans-port*	*Financial*	*Public administration Services Education commercial*
Arunachal	1993-1994	13.0	0	8.9	1.6	7.0	4.7	0	1.7	62.9
	1999-2000	19.9	0	0	0	2.6	34.3	0	0.5	42.7
Assam	1993-1994	1.3	3.9	10.4	0	1.1	4.0	0	2.0	77.2
	1999-2000	1.7	0	0.5	0.5	0.4	9.5	3.9	1.3	82.1
Manipur	1993-1994	19.1	0	29.7	0	0.5	26.0	0.3	1.8	22.6
	1999-2000	13.1	0	18.0	0	0.4	33.8	2.9	0.8	31.0
Meghalaya	1993-1994	2.1	0	3.4	0.5	5.0	33.2	1.0	0.8	53.9
	1999-2000	0.8	0	4.1	0	0.1	25.0	0.5	1.5	68.0
Mizora	1993-1994	51.9	0.1	3.7	0.2	0.8	22.0	0.3	0.1	20.
	1999-2000	41.5	1.2	3.0	0	3.9	24.5	0.7	1.4	23.8
Nagaland	1993-1994	10.6	0	0	1.4	6.3	6.4	0	0	75.2
	1999-2000	3.1	0	4.3	0	1.3	11.5	0	3.2	76.5
Tripura	1993-1994	3.6	1.0	3.4	0	4.1	2.4	0	1.9	83.
	1999-2000	2.3	0	4.2	0.1	3.1	10.7	2.7	1.7	75.3
India	1993-1994	19.3	0.7	23.6	0.3	4.9	10.7	1.5	2.2	36.6
	1999-2000	14.6	0.4	23.2	0.2	5.5	16.4	2.0	2.8	35.0

Source: NSSO 50th and 55th rounds

Table 7.7: Workers in Unorganized Services Sector in North Eastern States–Urban

	Arunachal	*Assam*	*Manipur*	*Meghalaya*	*Mizoram*	*Nagaland*	*Tripura*	*India*
HI	124	3201	114	751	120	1099	347	274760
H2	681	32924	5299	8220	2138	2703	4825	240133
	(38.4)	(27.1)	(29.1)	(45.1)	(27.3)	(30.7)	(21.2)	4(19.2)
11	-	661	119	93	8	16	151	18458
12	9	8579	2974	1111	1826	615	2269	127339
		(7.7)	(16.3)	(5.8)	(23.4)	(7.0)	(10.0)	2
13	8	18285	1795	229	16	336	4679	119720
		(15.1)	(9.8)				(20.6)	4
14	122	9998	320	1429	244	601	808	718379
	(6.9)	(8.2)		(7.4)		(7.0)		
K	30	8102	1895	1822	224	207	2785	161101
								I
M	374	17438	3954	1923	2386	1911	2637	220212
		(14.4)	(21.7)	(10.0)	(30.5)	(21.7)	(11.6)	7
N	102	10070	674	1194	135	328	1182	105229
		(8.3)		(6.2)			(5.2)	6

0	322	12118	1104	2414	721	989	3055	173121
		(10.0)		(12.6)	(9.2)	(I 1.2)	(13.4)	0
All	1772	12137	18213	19186	7818	8805	22737	124801
		5						71
Percentage to total urban workforce	2.3	11.2	8.2	14.7	3.7	7.8	13.0	13.6

* *Source:* Unorganised Service Sector in India, NSSO 57 Round, 2001-02

Code: H 1- Hotel, H2-restaurant, I I-storage and warehousing, 12- mechanized road transport, I3-other transport, 14- communication, K- real estate, renting and business activities, M- education, N- health and social work, 0- other community, social and personal services

* Figures in brackets are in percentage.

In Assam, Meghalaya and Tripura health related and social works also has emerged as one important service activities in the unorganized sector in urban areas. Apart from these other community, social and personal service activities are emerging as major activities in Assam, Meghalaya, Nagaland and Tripura. These kinds of prospective jobs in education, health and community services can be said upper end jobs requiring skill and educations. A comparative figure on the movements of such jobs from time series data could not be attained as the earlier NSSO round on this theme was conducted way back in 1979-80 and data for the region are not available. In the case of value added the restaurant and the transport sector accounts for about 60 percent of the total value added in the unorganized service sector in most of the states. The contribution of the education sector is also significant in the states.

Growth of workforce in urban areas reveals two definite trends. There is growth of some urban centric jobs those require technical degrees or higher level of education and some require mostly manual skill. At the present labour market some jobs are well paid whereas others are not and a clear demarcation in earning in two different set of activities are visible. A job in the information technology or insurance sector fetches income many times more than the manual job in construction sector or rickshaw pulling.

Now question arises—where our rural exodus shall find space in the urban labour market of the region? It is true that apart from growth of certain jobs in urban areas the rural poor themselves have tried to create their own living space in urban areas. All these however do not reflect that jobs are available in optimum number in urban spaces in north eastern region. The rise of urban unemployment particularly youth unemployment, underemployment and casualisation of workforce in urban areas of the region reflects that the job market in urban areas of north east is constrained and saturated. Table 7.8 reflects that during the short span of 1993-94 to 1999-2000 urban unemployment rate in all states of the region except in Tripura has shown a rising trend, whereas country as a whole this rate remains stagnant during 1993-94 to 1999-2000. Moreover, there is alarming rise of urban youth unemployment in the age group of 15 to 29 years (Table 7.9). Apart from the visible under-employment problem there is also rise of invisible under-employment in the region in recent times. The proportion of people who did not work more or less regularly throughout the year has shown considerable increase in urban areas in all states of the region (Table 7.10). Urban people in the eligible work age group available for additional and alternative works are in good proportions and these proportions are showing increasing trend in the states of Meghalaya, Mizoram, Nagaland and Tripura (Table 7.11 and 7.12). To supplement income and not having enough work were the reasons cited for seeking additional work. All means that present works are not remunerative enough. Overall all these reflect constraints in livelihood at the present urban labour market of north east India. These also have direct reflection on rapid casualisation of urban workforce in the region (Table 7.13). Now, unemployed, underemployed, casual workers and workers with unremunerative jobs together account for a significant proportion of people in urban areas of the region. On the other hand migration to urban areas in search of job is increasing and it has increasingly become difficult to accommodate the workers in the urban space.

Table 7.8: Urban Unemployment in the North Eastern States, Usual Status

States	*1993-94*			*1999-2000*		
	Male	*Female*	*Total*	*Male*	*Female*	*Total*
Arunachal	1.7	7.7	2.6.	1.4	10.0	2.9
Assam	6.2	28.9	9.7	9.1	22.3	11.3
Manipur	5.3	4.4	5.0	7.4	10.3	8.1
Meghalaya	1.3	3.2	2.0	3.4	6.8	4.6
Mizoram	0.5	0.5	0.5	4.4	2.6	3.8
Nagaland	6.9	7.0	6.9	9.3	10.8	9.7
Tripura	6.2	20.1	9.0	5.5	8.8	5.9
India	4.5	8.2	5.2	4.8	7.1	5.2

Source: NSSO 50th and 55th rounds

Table 7.9: Youth Unemployment 15-29 Age Group, in the Urban Areas of the North Eastern States, Usual Status

	1993-94			*1999-2000*		
States	*Male*	*Female*	*Total*	*Male*	*Female*	*Total*
Arunachal	3.0	12.9	5.3	9.1	18.5	11.9
Assam	17.0	49.8	24.5	22.2	45.0	26.6
Manipur	18.0	8.0	15.4	22.6	24.2	23.1
Meghalaya	5.3	11.0	7.5	11.9	17.7	14.3
Mizoram	1.6	1.4	1.5	12.7	6.0	10.3
Nagaland	17.5	8.3	15.4	31.1	23.3	28.3
Tripura	18.4	43.3	25.1	22.1	17.3	21.4
India	10.8	19.4	12.4	11.5	16.6	12.4

Source: NSSO 50th and 55th rounds

Table 7.10: Urban Underemployment in the North Eastern States, Usual Status

	1993-94			*1999-2000*		
States	*Male*	*Female*	*Total*	*Male*	*Female*	*Total*
Arunachal	7.6	4.2	7.2	40.1	37.8	39.8
Assam	1.9	1.6	1.8	3.2	1.8	3.0
Manipur	2.8	0.6	2.2	15.3	14.6	15.1
Meghalaya	0.3	1.9	0.7	4.0	5.8	4.6
Mizoram	1.2	1.5	1.3	17.7	17.6	17.7
Nagaland	1.4	-	1.2	3.3	6.4	4.0
Tripura	2.2	3.1	2.3	8.2	3.0	7.7
India	6.1	9.6	6.7	6.5	8.9	6.9

Source: NSSO 50th and 55th rounds

Table 7.11: Usually Working Person 15+ Age, available for Additional Work in Urban Areas of North Eastern States

States	*1993-94*			*1999-2000*		
	Male	*Female*	*Total*	*Male*	*Female*	*Total*
Arunachal	8.0	10.6	8.3	3.7	0.5	3.2
Assam	8.0	9.5	8.1	6.9	3.5	6.4
Manipur	7.5	9.3	8.0	4.4	6.1	4.9
Meghalaya	0.9	-	0.7	1.7	1.2	1.5
Mizoram	1.5	1.1	1.3	3.4	4.5	3.8
Nagaland	3.9	1.4	3.5	5.3	5.3	5.3
Tripura	0.9	0.3	0.8	1.5	3.7	1.7
India	4.4	5.1	4.5	6.1	5.8	6.0

Source: NSSO 50th and 55th rounds

Table 7.12: Usually Working Person 15+ age, available for Alternative Work in Urban Areas of North Eastern States

States	*1993-94*			*1999-2000*		
	Male	*Female*	*Total*	*Male*	*Female*	*Total*
Arunachal	7.8	10.5	8.3	2.0	1.6	1.9
Assam	6.9	12.1	7.4	7.1	7.3	7.1
Manipur	5.8	8.7	6.6	4.7	5.9	5.0
Meghalaya	1.5	3.8	2.1	2.8	1.2	2.3
Mizoram	1.8	1.6	1.8	5.2	6.1	5.5
Nagaland	2.7	0	2.3	7.4	11.7	8.4
Tripura	1.3	1.0	1.2	1.7	3.7	1.9
India	4.2	4.2	4.2	6.8	6.0	6.6

Source: NSSO 50th and 55th rounds

Table 7.13: Casualisation of Workforce by Usual Status in Urban Areas in North Eastern States

States	1993-94			1999-2000		
	Male	Female	Total	Male	Female	Total
Arunachal	8.5	9.1	8.5	19.4	7.2	16.9
Assam	9.9	24.4	11.6	11.2	20.6	12.5
Manipur	3.4	1.9	2.8	11.6	5.7	10.3
Meghalaya	9.6	12.1	10.3	19.2	13.5	17.4
Mizoram	7.4	1.6	5.4	17.5	15.1	16.4
Nagaland	6.6	-	5.9	4.6	1.5	3.8
Tripura	12.4	16.0	13.1	15.9	14.0	15.7
India	16.0	27.5	18.0	16.9	23.1	18.0

Source: NSSO 50th and 55th rounds

The data revealed by the NSSO are reflective enough that there is crisis in livelihood in urban areas of north east India. In such situation will the rural migrants find space to lead a decent living in urban areas? As we have seen urban labour market at present is showing two discerning trends - one is the categories of higher end jobs in public administrations, educational, health, financial services and informational technology sectors and the other is lower end jobs in construction works, transportation and in petty trades. It is true that certain jobs in the lower end labour market in urban areas will always be in demand considering the poor human development context. To enter the upper end jobs it requires certain skill and level of educational attainment whereas in the lower end jobs there is scope for relative easy entry with minimum investments.

Do the skill possessed by the rural migrants commensurate the skill required at the present urban labour market? The educational backgrounds of the people who have migrated from rural areas of the region to the urban areas for employment reveal poor level of educational attainment (Table 7.14). This means that just about one fifth of the migrants are capable of entering the upper end jobs in the urban labour market and most of the rural exodus simply turns to provider of labour supply to the lower end jobs in urban areas.

Table 7.14: Educational Attainment of the Intra-state Rural-Urban Migrants citing Employment as Reason for Migrants in NE States, 1991

States	*Matriculate*		*Graduates*		*Technical degree or diploma*	
	Male	*Female*	*Male*	*Female*	*Male*	*Female*
Arunachal	26.0	29.3	11.8	11.0	5.5	3.0
Assam	31.6	26.9	20.4	11.3	5.9	2.4
Manipur	20.5	29.6	18.2	17.4	2.7	1.4
Meghalaya	20.0	20.9	8.7	6.9	2.2	1.3
Mizoram	22.6	30.7	10.4	5.3	3.2	1.3
Nagaland	29.6	49.2	10.0	7.1	2.1	1.2
Tripura	23.0	15.7	15.4	8.2	3.9	1.1

Source: Census of India, 1991

The two kinds of segregated job markets based on educational attainment and skill development have created a huge difference in earning among the urban workers. There are some who earn a several hundred thousands a year and there are many who find it difficult to access the basic amenities of their daily life. There is scope to investigate whether the workers in the lower end labour market of urban areas of the region able to earn a decent income to meet their needs, including health and educational expenditure of their children.

The Committee on Fair Wages (1948) felt that the living wage should enable the worker to provide for her/himself and family, not merely the basic essentials of food, clothing and shelter but a measure for frugal comfort including education for children, protection against ill health, requirements of essential social needs and insurance against important misfortune, including old age. The committee was not sure how it could aim at or approach to this standard in the prevailing economic conditions. Taking Indian conditions into consideration, the committee was of the view that a minimum wage must provide not merely for the bare substances of life, but for the preservation of the efficiency of the workers. The members of the committee were unanimous that fair wage should on no account be less than the minimum wages (Report of National Commission on Labour, 2002). Table 7.15 could provide a picture the minimum amount a worker in urban space of north eastern region earns. It indicates that except in Arunachal the wages earned by the workers in urban spaces in the region are so less that it will not generate enough for a family of five to lead a decent life i.e., the earning is below the urban poverty line.

Table 7.15: Average Daily Wage in Rs. of Urban Casual Workers Engaged in Other than Public Work

States	*Male*	*Female*	*Total*
Arunachal	136.65	250.00	159.07
Assam	70.95	51.59	65.58
Manipur	71.22	40.90	65.86
Meghalaya	75.67	61.12	72.06
Mizoram	86.07	64.22	79.23
Nagaland	81.47	-	81.47
Tripura	60.78	46.21	59.12
India	62.26	37.71	56.96

Source: NSSO 50th and 55th rounds

Accessing the Basic Amenities in Urban Life

Considering the poor level of educational attainment and skill development we assume that the migrants to the urban areas in search of jobs enter the lower end job market and earn bare minimum. Are they able to get access to basic amenities in urban life? What is the state of affairs of basic urban services in the region? A look at the current status of basic amenities in urban areas of the region would provide us some indication about this. The concern for addressing this is how the movement of labour from rural areas has affected the quality of life in urban areas?

Data on status of urban basic amenities are available from the NSSO 54th round on Drinking water, sanitation and hygiene in India. However, data for hill states of the region are available at an aggregate level. Data reveal that considerable section of urban population in the region do not have access to sufficient and quality sources of drinking water supply, access to sanitary toilet and bathing space. Moreover, a good section of people in urban areas share in accessing their principal sources of water supply, latrine and bathrooms (Table 7.16 and 7.17). These inadequacies are more acute in the hill states of the region. All these are indicative that a good proportion of urban people in north east region do not have the access to quality urban life. The rapid urbanization process has believed to make the situation further aggravated.

Table 7.16: Status of Amenities in Urban Areas of North-Eastern Region

	HH not having DWS within the residential premise	*Reporting Insufficiency ofDWS in any month of the year*	*Unsatisfactory quality of DWS from principle sources*
Assam	22.3	1.8	36.4
NER	45.2	19.3	27.3
India	134.3	114.9	111.2

Table 7.17: Status of Basic Amenities in Urban Areas of North-Eastern Region

	Non-availability of bathrooms	*No latrine used*	*Use of unsanitary latrine*	*Sharing principle sources of*		
				DWS	*Bathroom*	*Latrine*
Assam	13.4	2.0	34.6	44.7	26.4	31.0
NER	39.9	2.4	48.1	64.0	24.5	37.2
India	35.3	25.5	33.0	58.7	24.7	37.1

Source: Drinking water, sanitation and hygiene in India 1999, NSSO 54th Round, 1998.

One issue emerges here is that at the present liberalized environment with the withdrawing tendency of the state from all public spheres including in the urban basic services, services are becoming available only for those who are capable of paying for these. The situation has emerged that the poor in lower end jobs in urban space with their minimum earning are not capable of using the basic services to lead a quality life. It is true that the legislation of minimum wages is incapable to address the wellbeing in such context. What is the way out at present in the urban labour market which currently shows a huge discrepancy in earning purely based on attainment of skill and education?

With two discernable trends in the labour market a larger section of worker find it difficult to avail all the basic urban amenities in order to lead a decent life with their minimum wages. The saturation of labour market along with requirement of minimum level skill and education to occupy the upper end of the job market led to underemployment and poor earning of many. The present trend shows a decline in the organized sector employment. How to address all these problems emergent at present and those likely to be aggravated in near future with rising flow of labour force from rural areas? Is it possible to limit the growth of urban labour market by reallocating labour in some specific sectors in rural areas? This could have been a better option but did not happen. Can education, skill development and training help the rural labour force to compete for the relatively upper end jobs and thereby bring some fairness in their earning? Or can we have a wage policy which will assure fair wages for all workers and thereby bring some equality? Or that there must be enough provision of basic urban services that everybody will have access to. All these are issues linked to address the questions of a better life for workers in the urban areas. However, at the present context of withdrawing tendency of the state all options are seemingly not possible and people are being compelled to pay for the services they avail.

It is true that our urban areas are not planned to accommodate the huge rural exodus. There may be some possibilities to reduce congestion in the urban space. It is true that some jobs are better performed in urban centres. Still there are possibilities of reallocating/creating some jobs away from main urban areas. There is wide scope to generate sufficient non-farm activities in the rural areas through appropriate policy supports. This could to a great extent prevent large-scale movement of people to urban centres at the lower end of the job market.

It is however also true that the urban areas will always require service of certain lower end jobs in construction, public works and infrastructural development. Basically these are the sectors experiencing tremendous growth in the recent times and the characteristic of these sectors is that growth of other sectors in the economy largely influences generation of jobs in these lower end sectors. It is true that through these lower end jobs, the unskilled (even the skilled) with the prevailing wage rate cannot expect to get the access to better urban services. It is also true that through an appropriate wage policy (which may be difficult to adopt at the present economic environment) and assurance of basic urban infrastructure and services it is possible to acquire access to basic services and maintain better human capital. All these are considering the unlimited labour supply at the lower end jobs in urban labour market.

In this context there is also possibility by generating better human capital with adequate skill development. Towards this end, reviewing comprehensively the lacunae in the present system of skill generation, the National Commission on Labour, 2002 has recommended a reorientation to evolve (a) a modular approach of vocational training to enable development in multi-skilling traits; b) a competency based training system linked to world of work; and c) a flexible competency-based certification system to provide for the recognition of skills in the large informally trained workforce. Strength of this system of training lies in its ability to generate trained manpower with a high degree of competence to suit the needs of a wide range of technologies and flexibility to cope with new technologies that would be expected to emerge in the future in the changing economic environment (Mathur and Mamgain, 2002). Apart from such skill training higher educational attainment in the sectors, which shows growth at the present economic environment, can also help the new entrants in urban areas to acquire job at the upper end urban job market and strengthen the bargaining power. The main thrust of the economic policy at present is on allowing free play of the market forces in determining how much and what should be produced in different sectors and the withdrawal of protective cover from competition. This implies relative shrinkages of celiain activities vis-a-vis activities in which expansion is envisaged. This in turn will require shifting of labour and workforce from declining to expanding sectors. The challenge for the workforce to assure a decent living at the present context is largely based on their capacity to adapt to the changing upper end urban labour market. Skill development and training would now play greater role in generating better human capital and access to urban basic services, including provision of health care and education assurance of a decent living in the urban areas. This is true, but the questions again remain - will everyone get opportunity to access education and skill development programme? What would be the role of the state in this context?

REFERENCES

Kannan, K.P. (2005), "Linking Employment Guarantee to Human Development," *Economic and Political Weekly*, October 15.

Mathur, A. and R.P. Mamgain (2002), "Technical Skills, Education and Economic Development in India," *Indian Journal of Labour Economics*, Vo!' 45, No.4.

Shara, R.K.S., Kumar and S. Meher (2002), *Indian Journal of Labour Economics*.

Report of the National Commission on Labour (2002), Ministry of Labour, Government of India.

in the third and fourth place, while Tripura stands sixth with 17 percent.

Objective, Scope & Methodology of the Study

The present study is an attempt to trace the process of urbanization in Tripura. Starting with the history of urbanization in Tripura, the paper focuses on the trends and volume of urbanization in Tripura. The degree, pace and tempo of urbanization are considered for attaining the above objective. Moreover, the paper will map out the pattern of urbanization and undertake a SWOT analysis to chalk out the issues and challenges to urbanization in Tripura and finally suggests some policy initiatives.

The study depends entirely on secondary data and Census publications are the major source. The standard mathematical estimations have been applied as and when required in the course of the study.

Historical Background to Urbanization in Tripura

The only municipal town of Tripura is its capital Agartala and this itself is an indicator regarding the echelon of urbanization in Tripura. However, the paradox is that the first attempt at the establishment of the Agartala Municipal Committee with the British Political Agent as the chair was made way back in 1871 by the Maharaja Bir Chandra Manikya. An act providing nominated members from the eight wards was further passed in 1874. Two other acts in support of municipal administration were passed in 1912 and 1939, but it was not until 1978 that Agartala had its first elected municipality.

Table 8.1 attests to the fact that till 1951 there was only one (1) urban area in the state, Agartala, which progressed from a Class V category town in 1931 to Class IV category town in 1941 and to Class III in 1951. During the period of 1951-1961, the number of towns increased to six (6) and it stayed still during the 1971 census. Interestingly, Agartala's population crossed the 100000 people mark in the same period and it qualified as a Class I town during the 1971 census itself. The

Table 8.1: Number of urban areas in Tripura during 1901-2001

Year	Class I	Class II	Class III	Class IV	Class V	Class VI	Total
1901					1		1
1911					1		1
1921					1		1
1931					1		1
1941				1			1
1951			1				1
1961			1	1	4		6
1971		1		4	1		6
1981		1	1	4	2	2	10
1991		1	4	7	4	2	18
2001		1	6	9	7		23

Source: Various Census Reports

number of urban areas in the state has since then progressed successively to 10 the extent of urban governance is extended to one municipal and 18 during the 1981 and 1991 census owing to the emergence of new and small urban agglomerations. Presently, council and twelve Nagar Panchayats. The census classification however in addition to these 13 urban areas considered another 10 Census towns for its classification of urban areas.

Table 8.2 shows that the extent of urbanization is maximum in the West district both in terms of the urban population and the number of urban areas. 26.75 percent of the population of the district are urbanites living in 13 towns or UAs and they account for 76 percent of the total urban population of the state. The North Tripura district has more urban population than the South Tripura district even though the number of urban areas is less. Dhalai district is in the lowest end of urbanization in the state. It should be noted here that there is significant positive

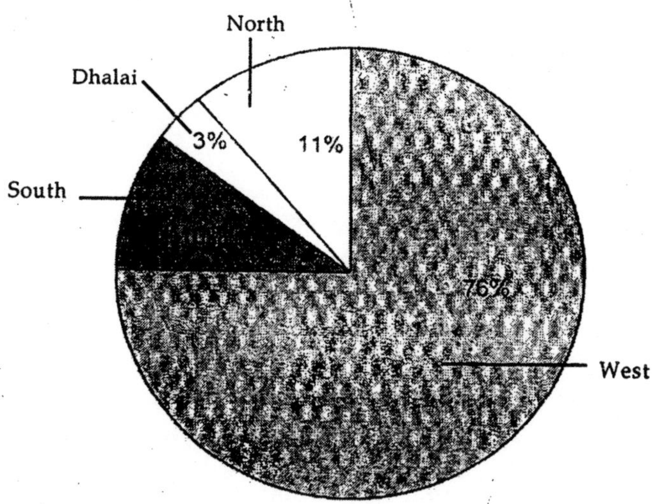

Fig. 8.1: District-wise break up of Urban Population in Tripura

Table 8.2: District-wise Urban Population, Number of Urban areas (UAs), & Human Development Index in Tripura

Sl. No.	*District*	*Total Population*	*Urban*	*No. of UAs*	*HDI*
1.	West Tripura	1532982	410067 (26,75)	13	0.62
2.	South Tripura	767440	54167 (7.06)	4	0.57
3.	Dhalai	307868	18867 (6.13)	3	0.51
4.	North Tripura	590913	62669 (10.61)	3	0.59
Total			3199203 0.59	545750 (57.05)	23

Source: THDR, 2007

Notes: Figures in parentheses indicate percent of Total population.

correlation between the degrees of urbanization and the Human Development Index. The Spearman 'rho' suggests a value of .975 which is significant at the .01 level, while Kedell's 'tau_b' value is .949, significant at .05 levels. Thus the human development indicators appear to be in a better state in the urban areas of Tripura.

Table 8.3 shows that total population of Tripura has increased by more than 18 fold over the past 100 hundred years, while the urban population and the rural population grew by 85 fold and 16 fold respectively. The decadal change has been highest during the period 1941- 51 for all the three categories while it was least during the immediate past period, ignoring the urban figures for the period 1901-1911.

Volume and Trend of Urbanization in Tripura

The previous section shows that Agartala had been the only urban area in the state till 1951 and it moved up a step in

Table 8.3: Population of Tripura by Residence, 1901-2001

Year	*Population*			*Decadeal Change (%)*		
	Total	*Urban*	*Rural*	*Total*	*Urban*	*Rural*
1901	173325	6415	166910			
1911	229613	6831	222782	32.48	6.48	33.47
1921	304437	7743	296694	32.59	13.35	33.18
1931	382450	9580	372870	25.63	23.72	25.67
1941	513010	17693	495317	34.14	84.69	32.84
1951	645707	42595	603112	25.87	140.74	21.76
1961	1142505	102997	1039508	76.94	141.81	72.36
1971	1556342	162360	1393982	36.22	57.64	34.10
1981	2053058	225568	1827490	31.92	38.93	31.10
1991	2757205	421721	2335484	34.30	86.96	27.80
2001	3199203	545750	2653453	16.03	29.41	13.61

Source: Various Census Reports.

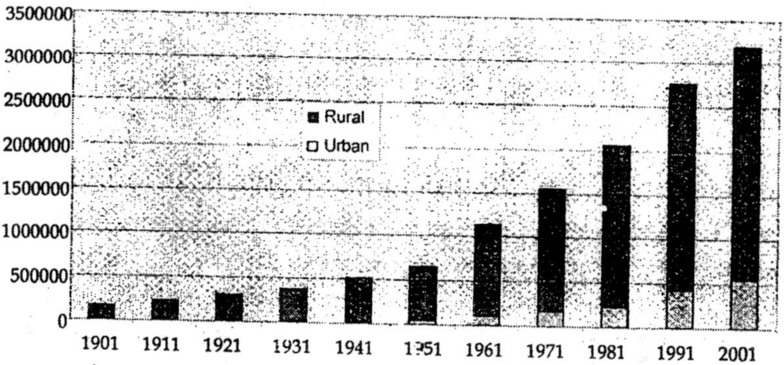

Fig. 8.2: Urban & Rural Composition of Popultion of Tripura

the town hierarchy during the period 1941 to 1951 possibly due to the partition of India and associated migration. However, the influx of the refugees had been maximum in the post-1951. People from the erstwhile East Pakistan came in large numbers and had a large role in the alteration of the demographic profile of the state and associated social fabric. Since 1971 Census onwards, the increase in the number of urban areas have also been a significant contributor to the increased urban population. Moreover, the insurgent activities have also been responsible for migration of rural people towards Agartala and its adjoining areas particularly from 1981 to 1991.

Degree of Urbanization

The degree or level of urbanization is defined as relative number of people who live in urban areas. Percent urban [(U/P)* 100] and percent rural [(R/P)*100] and urban-rural ratio [(U/R)*100] are used to measure degree of urbanization. These are most commonly used for measuring degree of urbanization. The ratio U jP has lower limit 0 and upper limit lies 0< U/P < 1. The index is 0 for total population equal to rural population. When whole population is urban, this index is one. When 50 percent of the population is rural, it means that there is one urbanite for each rural person. The urban-rural ratio has a lower limit of zero and upper limit 00 i.e O<U/R<oo. Theoretically

upper limit will be infinite when there is no rural population (R=O) but this is impossible.

Table 8.4 shows that the share of urban population has increased from 3.7 percent in 1901 to 17.06 percent in 2001, whereas the share of rural population shows a decrease from 96.30 percent in 1901 to 82.94 percent in 2001. Interestingly, we find the share of urban population decreasing marginally but continuously from the levels of 1901 till 1931 and even though it increased in 1941, it was well below the 1901 mark. The urban rural ratio for Tripura in 2001 was 20.57, which means that against every 100 rural people there are around 21 urbanites. This index shows a kind of stagnation during the period 1901 to 1941 and shows gradual increase since 1951, indicating the beginning of the acceleration phase in the process of urbanization. It may be noted here that the urban-rural ratio for India in 2001 was 38.47 (Datta, 2006) and India had passed through the present stage of Tripura, i.e. DR ratio =20.57, in 1951.

Table 8.4: Degree Index of Urbanisation

Year	*Urban Percent*	*Rural Percent*	*Urban-Rural ratio*
1901	3.70	96.30	3.84
1911	2.98	97.02	3.07
1921	2.54	97.46	2.61
1931	2.50	97.50	2.57
1941	3.45	96.55	3.57
1951	6.60	93.40	7.06
1961	9.02	90.98	9.91
1971	10.43	89.57	11.65
1981	10.99	89.01	12.34
1991	15.30	84.70	18.06
2001	17.06	82.94	20.57

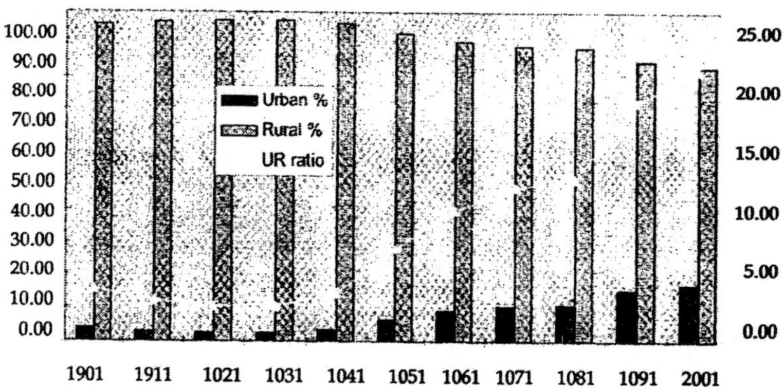

Fig. 8.3: Degree of Urbanization in Tripura

The inter-decadal annual exponential growth rate of urban population shows that in Tripura it grew fastest during the decade of 1951-1961 and was marginally higher than the rates prevailed in 1941-1951. Incidentally, the AGR for total population was also at its zenith during 1951-1961. Such a scenario is in sharp contrast to that of India because the lowest rate of growth in urban population for the whole country had been during 1951-1961. However, it is observed that the annual growth rates in the state have been fluctuating as the rates dropped for two successive decades and then increased during 1981-1991 again to drop.

The rural population growth rate in Tripura had been almost stagnant for the period 1901-1941. It declined during 1941-1951 and became the maximum for the period 1951-1961. Since 1961, the AGR for rural population has been decreasing slowly but surely and during 1991-2001, the rates were almost half of that of the preceding period. Throughout the course of urbanization, it is expected that rgup > rgtp > rgrp (Table 5), and in case of Tripura, such an observation is evident from 1931.

Table: 8.5: Annual Growth Rate (AGR) of Population by Residence

Year	*AGR (%) of Total Population (rgtp)*	*AGR (%) of Urban Population (rgup)*	*AGR (%) of Rural Population (rgrp)*
1901-1911	2.81	0.63	2.89
1911-1921	2.82	1.25	2.87
1921-1931	2.28	2.13	2.29
1931-1941	2.94	6.13	2.29
1941-1951	2.30	8.79	1.97
1951-1961	5.71	8.83	5.44
1961-1971	3.09	4.55	2.93
1971-1981	2.77	3.29	2.71
1981-1991	2.95	6.26	2.45
1991-2001	1.49	2.58	1.28

Source: Computed Various Census Reports

Notes: rgtp- growth rate of total population, rgup-growth rate of urban population & rgrp- growth rate of rural population

Tempo of urbanization refers to speed of urbanization and is measured as change registered in the level or degree of urbanization over the years. Table 8.6 suggests that tempo or speed of urbanization has not been a uniform in Tripura. Tempo of urbanization was negative from 1901 to 1931 and had since then been positive but fluctuated from a high of 6.49 during 1941-1951 to a low of 0.52 during 1971-1981. However, the tempo has slowed down during 1991-2001 as compared to 1981-1991. Fig: 8.4 attests to fluctuating nature of the tempo of urbanization and the fact that temp of rural proportion has been negative since 1931.

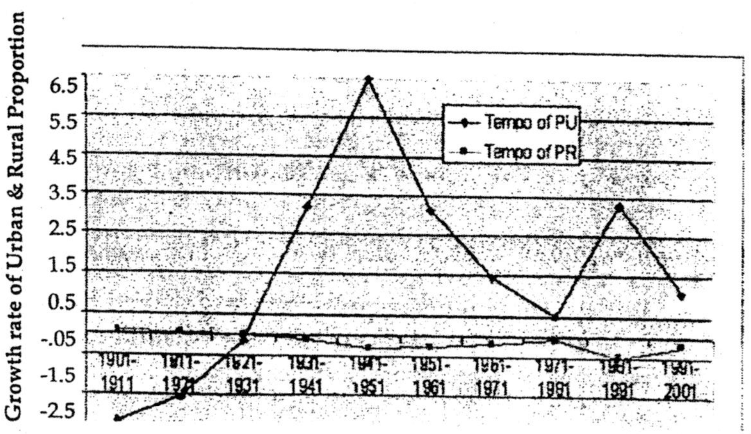

Fig. 8.4: Tempo of Urbanizaiton of Tripura, 1901-2001

Table 8.6: Tempo of Urbanization , 1901-2001

Year	*Growth rate Urban Proportion (Tempo of PU)*	*Growth rate Rural Proportion (Tempo of PR)*
1901-1911	-2.18	0.08
1911-1921	-1.57	0.04
1921-1931	-0.15	0.00
1931-1941	3.20	-0.10
1941-1951	6.49	-0.33
1951-1961	3.12	-0.26
1961-1971	1.46	-0.16
197 -1981	0.52	-0.06
1981-1991	3.31	-0.50
1991-2001 I	1.09	-0.21

Source: Computed

Notes: I.Tempo of PU = I/n [In (PU_{t+n} / PU_t)]* 100, where In = natural log, PU_{t+n} and PU_t = percent urban in t+n-th census and t-th census respectively, n = census interval= 10. *Tempo of PR = l/n [In $(PR_{t+n}$ /PR t] * 100, where In = natural log, PR_{t+n} and PR_t = percent urban in t+n th and t th census respectively, n= census interval= 10

Nature of Urbanization

It should be recalled here that the demographic profile of the state underwent a massive change due to the partition of India during independence and the following transition and turbulent years of the existence of East Pakistan and the consequent emergence of the new nation Bangladesh. The ethnic composition of the state has been changed and this fact has been responsible for insurgent and terrorist activities in Tripura. In other words, we say that the community character of the state and the man-land ratio have undergone a cavernous transformation owing to the influx of Bengali refugees from across the international border resulting in many social, economic and political miseries. As a result, Tripura still remains a state exhibiting most of the features of a backward economy.

Table: 8.7: Total Fertility Rates (TFR), Crude Birth Rates (CBR), Crude Death Rates (CDR) & Natural Growth Rates

	TFR (births/women aged 15-49 years)*		*CBR** per 1000 population*	*CDR** per 1000 population*	*NGR** per 1000 population*
	1998-99	*2004-05*	*2005*	*2005*	*2005*
Tripura	1.9	2.2	16.0	5.7	10.3
Urban	1.4	1.7	13.8	5.8	8.0
Rural	2.0	2.3	16.5	5.7	10.7

Source: * NHFS-2 1998-99 & NHFS-3 2005-06; ** SRS Bulletin (Oct, 2006).

Urban growth (Bhagat, 1992) generally occurs from three major factors—a) Natural increase, b) Net migration and c) Areal reclassification and Tripura is no exception. Since, data on the individual component of urbanization are not available, it would be erroneous to estimate any figures as such therefore we analyse the components of urbanization on the basis of the general economic framework of the state. Natural increase has been the most dominant form of urbanization in India for the period 1971-1981 & 1981-91 (Pathak & Mehta, 1995). In Tripura however, Table 8.7 shows that TFR, CBR & the NGR are higher for the rural areas while the CDR is higher for urban areas.

Thus, it is more likely that other factors have been more Responsible for urbanization.

Table 8.8 shows that of the total urban population, 228980 people and 41.96 percent are migrants by the Census classification of by place of last residence. It is understood that migration has been a major component of urbanization in Tripura and almost 74 percent of the urbanites in Tripura have migrated to their present place of enumeration from within the country itself. To be more specific, around 68 percent have migrated from other parts of the state while 6 percent had earlier been residents of other states of India. About 11 percent of the urban population in Tripura are from across the border and accounts for 26 percent of the urban migrants. Interestingly, the total number of international migrants in the state is 299813 and they form around 9.37 percent of the total population, which suggest that the net migration from other countries is skewed towards urban areas. Others have been identified as the major cause of migration by urban migrants of Tripura and others here include economic causes like poverty, natural causes like floods and earthquakes, political causes like insurgency and etc. (Bhowmik, 2006). Further, migration due to positive factors like work, business and education are comparatively low in Tripura.

Table 8.8: Migrants in Tripura (Place of Last Residence), 2001

Sl. No	*Type*	*Migrants*
1.	Total	961653
2.	Rural	732673
3.	**Urban**	**228980**
3.1	Domestic	169357
3.1.1	Intra-State	155307
3.1.2	Inter-State	14050
3.2	International 59623	

Source: Census, 2001

Notes: 1= 2+3; 3= 3.1+3.2 & 3.1= 3.1.1+3.1.2

Reclassification of urban areas has been on -going over the years as is evident in Table 1. Presently, there are 23 urban areas, an increase of 5 units over the 1991 census arising from the inclusion of four new areas and bifurcation of an existing one. The 2001 Census saw an increase of 124029 persons in the urban area and of that 27.72 percent was catered by the new areas while the major 72.28 percent of the increase was contributed by the growth in the older urban areas. As seen before, urban areas in Tripura include 10 Census Towns and 8 of these are situated in the West Tripura district. Three of these CTs have been incorporated to the Agartala municipality in 2004 and the remaining five are also in the fringes of Agartala city.

The process of urbanization in Tripura therefore does not show any definite pattern. Industrialization being almost non-existent, the growth process has been slow and there has been no real big-push of migration from the rural agricultural sector to the urban industrial sector. The major economic theories of migration which lead to urbanization in general have not been in operation in the state. The state has a powerful and dominant public administration system and often the process of urbanization has been led by the growth of the public administration. Almost all the urban units leaving aside those on the suburb of Agartala are administrative headquarters and thus have benefited and progressed to being an urban area. In other words, the pull of the urban sector has been less dominant than the rural push that often arises out of poverty.

Agartala's dominance in the urbanization process of Tripura has been phenomenal though its share in the total urban population has been declining over the years – 100 percent in 1951, 61.75 percent in 1971 and 34.81 percent in 2001. Majority of the focus of the urban development has been on Agartala though efforts have been taken to spread out the urban facilities and programmes throughout the state. One of the associated factors of urbanization is the growth in property and real estate prices and the rates in Agartala are almost at par with other major Indian cities. The high land price has resulted in fragmentation of the residential area and emergence of tiny plots.

Considering the periods of higher urbanization in the sociopolitical time line, we find negative factors like refugees, ethnic classes, and threats of insurgency contributing significantly towards growth in urban population. Thus the major features of urbanization in Tripura are-

- Urbanization occurring without industrialization and formation of strong economic base
- Public administration led urbanization occurring
- Distress migration and internal displacement led urbanization
- Lopsided urbanization with growth in the capital city and its suburbs
- Though poverty induced, proportion of slums is less though the total numbers of slum dwellers are growing at an increasing rate.

Moreover, the other common problems of urban life in the country like-water supply, traffic congestion, drainage and sanitation, water and air pollution are also evident in Agartala. However to be more specific we undertake the SWOT analysis as below:-

Strengths:

- High levels of some human development indicator, particularly education and literacy
- Satisfactory levels of law and order in urban areas
- Financial support from international agencies
- Dynamic and pro-active urban governing bodies
- Favourable climate and environment
- Growing infrastructure- roads, street lighting.

Weakness:

- Lack of technical expertise in urban development
- Absence of large scale private sector enterprises
- Dearth in employment generating opportunities

- Shortage of industrial activities
- Poor electric power scenario
- Limited entertainment and amusement facilities
- High vehicle density and associated traffic problems.

Opportunities:

- Potential for border trade
- Utilization of natural gas
- Rubber based industrial units
- BPO and Call centres- educated and English knowing manpower
- Bamboo and Cane resources.

Threats:

- Unscientific and unhygienic garbage disposal and waste management system
- Lack of underground sewerage system
- Gradual decay in the water carrying capacity of the Howra & Gumti Rivers
- Unplanned growth of housing and buildings, narrow roads even carrying a patient in stretcher becomes tough
- Illegal filling up of ponds, crisis during fires
- Exorbitant land prices- emergence of land mafia.

Conclusion

The process of urbanization in Tripura has just crossed its infancy and still has miles to go before it matures, yet the various features as evident above calls for certain policy initiative. The state government has launched its programme 'N agaradoy' in all the 13 urban bodies all over the state to facilitate decentralized urban planning and to provide better civic amenities and services to the people living in urban areas and for improving the quality of life, environment and economic condition.

Yet some more policy initiatives like- a) redirection of

investment to develop a strong economic base for Agartala and other urban areas, b) integration of the rural and urban economy with emphasis on plantation and horti-based industries, c) extension in the coverage of the Integrated Development of Small and Medium Towns (IDSMT), d) amalgamation of short and medium term plans with the long term perspective plans, e) development of Urban Development Authorities with more executive powers would boost the levels of urbanization and also contribute significantly to the overall development process of the state.

REFERENCES

Bhagat, RB. (1992), "Components of Urban Growth in India with Reference to Haryana: Findings from Recent Censuses," *Nagarlok*, Vol. 25, No.3.

Bhowmik, I (2006), *Migration Profile of Tripura*, Presentation at the Census Data Dissemination Workshop, BBM College, Agartala.

Brockerhoff, M. (1999), Urban Growth in Developing Countries: A review of Projections and Predictions, *Population and Development Review*, Vol 25. No. 4.

Datta, P. (2006), Urbanisation in India, Regional and Sub-Regional Population Dynamic Population Process in Urban Areas, European Population Conference.

Davis Kingsley and Golden H.H. (1954), Urbanisation and development in pre-Industrial Areas, *Economic Development and Cultural Change*, Vol.3, no 1.

Davis Kingsley (1962), Urbanisation in India - Past and Future, in Turner, R (ed.) *India's Urban Future*, University of California Press, Berkeley.

Davis, K. (1965), The urbanization of the human population, *Scientific American*, 213(3)

National Commission on Urbanisation (1988), Report of the National Commission on Urbanisation, Vol II, August, Ministry of Urban Affairs, Govt. of India

Pathak, P and Mehta, D. (1995), Recent Trend in Urbanisation and Rural-Urban Migration in India: Some Explanations and Projections, *Urban India*, vol. 15, No.1, pp.1-17.

Premi, M. K. (1991), India's Urban Scene and Its Future Implications, *Demography India*, 20(1).

Registrar General (1991) *Census of India*, General Population Tables Tripura, Series 24 Part II-A

Registrar General, 2001: *Census of India*, 2001, India, 2A, Mansingh Road, New Delhi 110011, 25th July, 2001

Sen, A. and Ghosh, J. (1993), *Trends in Rural Employment and Poverty Employment Linkage*, ILO-ARTEP Working Paper, New Delhi

Sovani, N. V. (1966), *Urbanisation and Urban India*, Asia Publishing House, Bombay.

Tripura Darpan (2007) Tathyapanji-O- Nirdeshika.

9

Urbanization in Assam—A Case Study of Jagiroad Town

Purushottam Bhandari & H.C. Gautam

Introduction

Urbanization is a global phenomenon. It means living/situated in towns or cities. The definition of' 'urban' as applied in 2001 census include - (I) (a) All places with a municipality, corporation, cantonment board or notified town area committees, etc; (b) All other places which satisfied the following criteria - (I) A minimum population of 5,000 (II) Atleast 75 percent of the male population engaged in non-agricultural pursuits and (III) A density of population of at least 400 per sq.km. (1,000 per sq.mile); and (2) A district/sub-division/tahsil headquarters, if it is not statutory town, need to be treated as a census town only if it satisfies the demographic criteria mentioned in para I (b) above. Urbanization is a process of socio-economic-politico- and cultural change from the feudal society /medieval period's organization to capitalist mode of production. Prof. W.A. Lewis argues that "economic growth in necessarily associated with urbanization". It is related to industrialization and prosperity of a nation. Urbanization requires the economic needs of the people, local technology foundation, skill formation and overall absorption capacity of the system. In a nutshell, it promotes national economy development.

Area of the Study Region: The people of Jagiroad are originally Austric, Tibeto-Burmese, Dravidian and Aryan race. The main community of Jagiroad is Tiwa (Lalung). Other communities which migrated to Jagiroad for trade and commerce or employment avenues are Bodos, Koch, Chutia, Ahom, Brahmin, Muslim, Bihari, Marwari, Nepali, Bengali etc. A section of the population from Tiwa community has taken their occupation as dry fish selling. The occupational patterns of the people of Jagoroad are employees of HPC, employees of various government departments, educational institutions, petty cultivators, dairy farming, piggery, agricultural labourers, firewood cutters and sellers, industrial labourers etc.

Objectives of the Study: The paper addresses the following aspects:

(a) To study the parameters of urbanization

(b) To identify the areas associated with urbanization

(c) To examine the problems associated with urbanization

(d) To relate the degree of exploitation of tribal community

(e) To suggest policy recommendations for sustainable urbanization.

Sources of Data and Methodology: This paper is based on primary and secondary data. Reference has been made wherever specifically quoted. The requisite materials for historical prospective has been drawn from various sources and unpublished theses. Population data related to urban-rural distribution, sex ratio, growth rate, literacy rate, occupational pattern etc. has been taken from various volumes/series of 1991 and 2001 census of India. Secondary data are collected from panchayats, electricity board, telephone exchange, Sita Jakhala Dugdha Utpadak Samabai Samiti, Veterinary department, hospitals, educational institutions, Mayong Development Block, Sub-Divisional Economic and Statistical Department, Economic Survey - Assam 2001-2002, Statistical Hand Book - Assam 2002 etc.

Importance of Urbanization: The importance of urbanization at Jagiroad is sketched as follows:

- Employment avenues to the low income brackets,
- Self-employment facilities to various enterprises,
- Facilitated entry of the middle class in the organized sector,
- Investment opportunities,
- Access to higher education, and
- Access to better health services.

Urbanization in Assam

Urbanization process in Assam started since time immemorial. During the reign of Pratap Singh (1603-41) two markets were established at Dopdar and Borhat to encourage trade with the Nagas. Ahom monarch established a large number of marts in places like Bebejia, Janji, Titabar, Nazira & Simaluguri. In course of time, these marts were converted into small towns. The towns of Gauhati and Hajo were highly urbanized centres and had trading connections with the Western Gateway of Assam. The people of Bhutan used to come to the Valley of the Manas River via Tasgong and Dewangiri to Hajo and exchanged Yak-tails, lac, woolen, salt, silk, muga, cotton clothes and dried fish. It was estimated that at the close of the nineteenth century, the trade with Bhutias was worth about Rs.2 lakhs. Sadiya was an important township where Assamese, Tibetan and Chinese merchants exchange their goods. The trading items of Sadiya mart were various kinds of clothes, salt, swords, spears, ivory musks etc.

Traditionally, urban units are classified into six classes on the basis of their population pattern. These were i) Class I - population 1,00,000 and above; ii) Class II -population 50,000 - 99,999; iii) Class III - population 20,000 - 49,999; iv) Class IV -population 10,000 - 19,999; v) Class V- population 5,000-9,999 and vi) Class VI-population less than 5,000.

In 1901, the number of towns/urban agglomerations was 12 and increased to 74 in 1991 census. The class I towns of 1991 census were Guwahati Municipal Corporation, Dibrugarh MB, Silchar MB and Jorhat MB. Number of towns merged/declassified after 1991 are 5. These are Niz Hajo,Amingaon in Kamrup

District, Raha in Nagaon District, Jogighopa Paper Mill in Bongaigaon District and Jagiroad Paper Mill in Morigaon District. The number of towns in Assam in 2001 census was 80. The number of census towns in 2001 was 45. The population of 6 towns/urban agglomerations in 2001 census are Guwahati Municipal Corporation (8,14,575), Dibrugarh MB (1,32,597), Silchar MB (1,56,740), Jorhat MB (1,14,065), Nagaon MB (1,08588) and Tinsukia MB (1,01943). This is shown in the map. The progress of urban population of the state and districts during 1991-2001 is given in the table 9.1.

Population Growth Pattern

Urbanization of Jagiroad includes both Jagiroad (CT) and HPC (CT).The population of Jagiroad (CT) was 13,582 persons - 7,430 males and 6152 females in 1991 census. Sex ratio (females per 1,000) of Jagiroad (CT) in 1981 was 828. The population of Jagiroad Paper Mill (CT) was 3,790 persons - 2,092 males and 1,698 females in 1991. Sex ratio of Jagiroad Paper Mill (CT) was 812 in 1991.Jagiroad Paper Mill (CT) was declassified in 2001 census. The population of Jagiroad as per 2001 census was 17,254—9371 males and 7,883 females. The decadal growth (1991-2001) was 26.77%. Sex ratio was 841 in 2001 census.

Gender Dimension

Urbanization process provides better employment avenues and income to the women folk. It also generates better basic services like education, health, water supply, sanitation, electricity, telephone facility, supply of L.P.G. to women community. The women of Jagiroad are better off in comparison to their counterparts in rural villages of Morigaon Districts like Hatimuria, Pakariguri, Hatibhange, Pabitara P.G.R., Barpak Jungle, Sildudi Gaon, Barkurani, Garakhiadhap, Kuranibari, BarDalani, Jhargaon, Lecheripam, Monaha Kacharigaon, Barsoloni Pathar, Barkoloi Pathar, Bangthaigaon, Bamungaon, Pachimnagaon, Kamerkuchi, etc. Urban population of Morigaon District in 1991 census was 1.33 percent and declined to 1.12 percent in 2001. Sex ratio (females per 1,000 males) of urban population of Morigaon District was 847 in 1991 that increased to 879 in 2001. Literacy rate of urban population of

Table 9.1: Progress in Urban Population of the State and Districts during 1991 - 2001

Sl.No.	Name of state/ district	Urban population 1991	2001	Percentage decadal growth
1	2	3	4	5
1.	Assam	2,487,795	3,389,413	+36.24
2.	Kokrajhar	50,724	63,632	+25.45
3.	Dhubri	161,981	190,546	+ 17.63
4.	Goalpara	52,096	67,289	+29.16
5.	Bongaigaon	73,854	110,287	+49.33
6.	Barpeta	97,318	125,140	+28.83
7.	Kamrup	655,215	900,518	+37.44
8.	Nalbari	23,475	27,478	+ 17.05
9.	Darrang	63,984	73,844	+ 15.41
10.	Morigaon	32,989	38,061	+15.37
11.	Nagaon	205,722	277,921	+ 35.10
12.	Sunitpur	103,908	147,831	+42.27
13.	Lakhimpur	49,130	65,129	+32.56
14.	Dhemaji	8,891	39,330	+342.36
15.	Tinsukia	158,674	224,174	+ 141.28
16.	Dibrugarh	183,580	219,976	+ 19.83
17.	Sibsagar	65,689	97,101	+47.82
18.	Jorhat	133,032	170,648	+28.28
19.	Golaghat	48,839	79,156	+62.08
20.	Karbi Anglong	70,466	92,751	+31.63
21.	N.C. Hills	34,486	58,079	+68.41
22.	Cachar	119,224	201,418	+68.94
23.	Karimganj	60,381	73,547	+21.80
24.	Hailakandi	34,138	45,557	+33.45

Soruce: Census of India 2001

Morigaon District was 85.84 percent – male 90.86 percent and female 80.05 percent as per 2001 census. The literacy rate of Jagiroad was 74.92 percent - male 79.99 percent and female 68.99 percent in 2001. However, it is observed in field survey that the Tiwa women of Jagiroad are not better of in comparison with the women of other communities because they have to do hard labour to support their families due to financial constraint.

Growth of Formal and Informal Sector

The World Bank and the International Labour Organization (ILO) have coined the terms 'formal' and 'informal' sectors to denote the fragmented labour market of the Third World Countries. Social scientists have introduced new terms to the fragmented labour market of underdeveloped countries by calling them 'organized' and 'unorganized' sectors or 'capital-intensive' and 'Labour-intensive' Sectors. The Registered Factories Act, the Shop & Establishments Act the Societies Registration Act are not applicable to informal sector. In India, approximately 50% of the urban population depends for their livelihood to informal sector. The formal sector of Jagiroad includes HPC, Cooperative societies, hospitals, educational institutions, banks, electricity board, PWD office, telephone exchange, railway station, Lahoti company, A.S.T.C., veterinary departments, insurance,.jute bag production unit etc. The formal sector of Jagiroad has certain distinct characteristics like (i) Adoption of capital-intensive or intermediate technology, (ii) High value of fixed asset per workers, (iii) Very high volume of capital available; (iv) large volume of products, (v) Organized, trained, skill and educated labour force, (vi) provision of bank credit and government assistance, (vii) better quality of raw-materials, (viii) better advertisement facility, (ix) domination of the entire economy, and (x) high profit margin. The workers of informal sector of Jagiroad town earn their bread by pursuing low grade and low productive economic activities like domestic works, rickshaw-pulling, thelia-pulling, loading and unloading, wood cutting, tailoring, repairing, weaving, pottery, basket making, grass cutting, indigenous transport , cobbling, construction work, fire wood selling, vending, hawking, blacksmith, handmade chalk manufactures etc. Informal sectors have certain distinct features like (i) employment per unit is minimal (ii) low credit facility (iii) low wages (iv) subordinated and dominated (v) relationship of customers is personalized and (vi) it is locally integrated. The informal sector of Jagiroad is operated by poor, underprivileged and illiterate. They do not have sufficient land assets, resources for investment, technical knowledge and administrative patronage. They do not demand employment avenues, shelters and other basic facilities but they create these facilities by their hard labour. They support the urbanization process by providing cheap labour and low priced goods and services. The formal sector expands functions and grows under the patronage of informal sector.

Growth of Dual Economy

According to Prof. William Arthur Lewis in his masterpiece, *The Theory of Economic Growth* (1955), the growth of urban economies of the Third World Countries is dualism in character. The process of urbanization in Jagiroad has created a dual economy consisting of modern sector like paper production, dry fish market, milk production, manufacture of jute bags, etc and traditional agriculture and handloom sector on the other. The co-existence of the modern and traditional sector perpetuates inequalities in income distribution. Due to the widening of gap between two sectors, large sections of urban population of Jagiroad are excluded from the modern capitalist sector.

Infrastructural Support System of Urbanization

The infrastructural support system of urbanization are discussed under the following headings:-

a) *Banking Facilities*: With a population of 17,254 as per 2001 census, Jagiroad is fortunate to have 5 bank branches in the entire locality. These are – (i) S.B.I., Jagiroad, (ii) S.B.I. Sonaikuchi/Kagajnagar, (iii) Canara Bank, (iv) Lakhimi Gaoliya Bank, (v) The Assam Co-operative Apex Bank Ltd. Three branches of these banks are computerized. The average annual loan disbursed by these banks amounted to Rs. 4 crore to Rs. 5 crore.

b) *Educational Facilities*: Urbanization facilitates access to better educational facilities. Education, general or technical, is the important factor that determines the economic quality of people. It is the most valuable of all capital. Any expenditure on it may be treated as national investment and must be taken into account while measuring capital formation. If one of the major goals of nearby all societies is rapid economic growth, then programme of human resources development must be designed to provide knowledge, skills and incentives required by a productive society. In a small township of Jagiroad, there are 10 LP schools, 7 ME schools, 4 high schools, 3 higher secondaries and 1 degree college.The high schools of Jagiroad are Girls High School, Bapuji High School, Joti Niwas High School and Rly. High School. The Higher secondary schools of the locality are Jagiroad Higher Secondary, Lakhi Deka School and Kendriya Vidyalaya (HPC). The lone college of the locality is Jagiroad College. It was established in 1979 with a student strength of 55, now has enrollment of 1345 students in 2004.

c) *Heath Services*: The health services available at Jagiroad are comparatively better in comparison to other urban areas of Assam. There are four hospitals at Jagiroad viz. Nakhola hospital, Rly, Hospital, HPC Hospital and a mini hospital for industrial workers. The number of private practitioner doctors is about 30. Doctors from Guwahati also visit for practice in private clinics in the locality.

d) *Urban electrification*: It has been stated that the quantity of electricity is an index of material development of living. Therefore, importance of power and energy in a developing society needs not be exaggerated. It is a basic input required to sustain economic growth and to provide basic amenities of life. As an instrument of socio-economic change in urban areas, electricity is considered not only a social amenity but also a key infrastructure of urbanization and urban development strategy. It has been found during field visit that there is irregular supply of electricity in Jagiroad township. Some households have to remain without light for many days. Moreover, the poor families of Jagiroad could not get their houses electrified as they have no residential houses of required standard for electrification. High installation cost also stands as a barrier in this regard. In this connection, it has been said that limited availability of the resources in the hands of the Government makes it impossible and impracticable to provide electricity to all houses of the town. As an alternative system, solar energy should be given priority in some of the areas of the town. According to Sub-Divisional Electricity Office, Jagiroad, 3 villages of the town which are electrified are as follows i) Nakhola Grant (Karkatbasti) - 135 households (62.79%), (ii) Nakhola -242 households (21.45%) and (iii) Ghunacha - 131 households (12.11 %).

e) *Telecommunication Facilities*: Telecommunication is an integral part of infrastructure to uplift economic development and promote faster social progress. In Assam, during 1998-99, number of telephone exchanges were 366, telephone stations 22, 84, 92 and telephone working connections (DELs) 211,906. In the same period, public telephone includes: long distance telephone (13,355) Gram Panchayat Public Telephone (2119), Local Public Telephone (962) and STD Public Telephone (3761). There is a telephone exchange at Jagiroad. As per the telephone Directory 2000 corrected up to 31-3-2000 (Nagaon Telecom District), the number of telephone connections at Jagiroad 393. At present mobile facilitiy is available at Jagiroad. Internet facility is also assessible nowadays.

f) *Water Supply*: According to UN-HABITA estimates, 60% of the world population will be living in urban areas by 2005. It will create water problem in urban areas. As per World Bank Study, there are 27 Asian Cities where in terms of hours of water availability is worst performer. In Indian cities, water is available for only of 2-8 hours a day. Water scarcity cities of India are Chennai, Delhi, Mumbai and Kolkata. Per capita water consumption in urban areas of India ranges between 40-300 liters per day. It is estimated that 15% of urban population of India do not enjoy safe drinking water facilities.

The main sources of water supply to the Jagiroad township are kucca wells, tube wells, wells and tape water. There is irregular settlement of people in the old railway tract and in the Sunaikuchi Hill. These are water scarcity areas. There is lack of sanitary latrines and drainage system in these areas. The growth of 'slum type' and squatter settlement of people in railway lands and forest land at Jagiroad are unhygienic and affected by rain and flood water. These are the places of the carriers of diseases like diarrhoea, dysentery and cholera. Infant mortality rate is also high in these areas.

g) *Transport facilities*: The transport facilities available at Jagiroad are both road transport and railway transport. Guwahati City of Assam is only 56km. from Jagiroad. The distance of Nagaon district is 67 km. from here. The district headquarter Morigaon is only 22 km. from Jagiroad. Since National Highway 37 passes through Jagiroad, it is possible to go either upper or lower Assam from Jagiroad. Railway train provides facilities to travel to Nagaon, Lumding, Dibrugarh, Guwahati etc. Taxi operators are available at Jagiroad Township.

h) *Market System*: Jagiroad is a trading centre for the people of the North East states for the purchase of dry- fish. A large dry fish market is situated here. It is one of the largest dry fish wholesale markets in Asia. Weekly and daily markets exist at Jagiroad. The people from Nellie, Amlighat, Bangfore, Jagibhakat Gaon, Jhargaon, Buraburi, Bardoloni, etc. use to visit Jagiroad regularly for trade and commerce purpose.

i) *Housing Facilities*: Urbanization demands more houses for accommodation for the increasing population. Housing shortage in urban India was about 7.57 million units in 1997. It is estimated that 12 million residents in Mumbai are slum dwellers or homeless. Jagiroad is also facing housing problem. Therefore, there is a tendency among some people to construct two or three storeyed houses. HDFC and HUDCO are providing housing loans to the salaried people. SBI, Canara Bank and LIC are also providing housing loans. A large number of houses to the urban poor of Jagiroad are constructed through Indira Awaas Yojana (IAY). There is lack of proper planning in the housing sector of Jagiroad area.

Sports Facilities

There is a mini-stadium at Jagiroad under the Jagiroad Sports Association. There are three playgrounds at Jagiroad viz. HPC playground, Jagiroad. Higher secondary school playground and Sapna Mazika playground. There are a few clubs at Jagiroad namely Kishore Club, Vivekananda Club, Jagiroad Sports Club, Jagiroad Health Club etc. In addition to this, there is an adventure group namely "Friends Circle" functioning at Jagiroad.

Growth of Consumerism

Urbanization promotes consumerism. There is increase of demand for goods and services because of the increase in the income level of the people. Consumers' demand depends on income level, preference, tastes, habit and availability of consumer credit. The process of urbanization at Jagiroad has created certain aspects of life style and behaviour pattern among the people. Affluent class of town area has more access to two-wheelers, cars, colour T.V., Mobile, telephone facilities, computer set, refrigerator, washing machine etc.

Beneficiaries of Urbanization Process: The urbanization process of Jagiroad does not serve the interest of the general population and state economy. The beneficiaries of urbanization process at Jagiroad are as follows:-

(i) Urban property owners

(ii) Educated class

(iii) Better off people with resources

(iv) Employees of H.P.C.

(v) Businessmen

(vi) Skill and technical knowhow persons
(vii) Private transport operators
(viii) Contractors
(ix) Affluent groups
(x) Employees of various institutions/organizations.

Tiwa Identity Crisis

The Hindustan Paper Corporation (HPC), a public sector undertaking, was set up in 1979 at Jagiroad and commercial production was started in the month of October 1985. A large area of tribal population was taken off by the HPC for the establishment of the mill. Tiwa population instead of getting employment and to improve the quality of life as a result of mill was uprooted economically, socially, politically, culturally and ecologically. They were permanently thrown out of their traditional pursuits of agriculture, handloom, forestry and wood-gathering.. Tiwa community's Miyadi Patta land was permanently annexed without paying compensation. Their agricultural and forest lands were clear off and the ecology of the area was destroyed. Penetration of capitalist economy in Tiwa dominated area of Jagiroad, enhanced by the railroad connectivity to different districts of Assam and armed with technicians, engineers, bureaucrats, contractors, doctors, teachers, lectures, investors, businessman from outside completely wiped out their indigenous economic activity. The Tiwa society was marginalized in the urbanization process and they were thrown out from their own locality. This creates Tiwa identity crisis. The HPC benefits only a handful of contractors, businessmen, hoteliers, private transport operators, employees and renters' class.

Growth of unemployment Problem

There is a steady growing unemployment problem at Jagiroad. The closing down of Spun Silk Mill and Polyester Mill have thrown out more than 600 people out of jobs. This generates industrial unemployment in the area. There is also growth of educated unemployment problem in the area. Setting up small scale industries and micro- enterprises will provide relief to the unemployed people of the area.

Environment Problem

i) *Depletion of Forest Resource*: Forest is a renewable resource of Assam. At the end of March 2000, the total forest area of Assam was 26130.58 sq. km out of which the state reserved forest area was 17421.94 sq. km. Total geographical area under National Parks and Wildlife Sanctuary is 2,219 sq. km. At present total area under encroachment is 59,100 hectares. The state has lost more than 409 sq. km. of forest area in the last decade. The forest wealth of Jagiroad is available on Sunai Kushi Reserve Forest. The excessive use of forest wealth at Jagiroad resulted depletion of forest resource of the area. There are approximately 100 woodcutters. There are lumbers, fire wood collectors, hand stone crushers and sand collectors of Sapna Mazika Nizara from the adjacent forest of Jagiroad. The Supreme Court of India has banned the operation of all the saw mills located in the forest area of the Northeast region in its order on December 12, 1996. The Sawmill of Jagiroad was closed but the valuable forest is unsafe at the hand of unscrupulous contractors, forest personnel, house builders, politicians and bureaucrats. In the recent study, it is found that 100 people live entirely on firewood collection on daily basis from the forest of Jagiroad and the earning made by these firewood collectors is estimated to be Rs. 5,000 per day. Every year in June, Beel Mela, a big furniture market flourishes which fetches thousand of rupees to the business communities. Further, there is considerable depletion of valuable flora and fauna of the forest of Sonaikuchi.

ii) *Paper Mill – A Threat to the Eco-System:* The main raw material for paper mill is bamboo. Bamboo plays an important role in the lives of the people viz. as a resource of construction materials, food, fodder, fuel and fencing material. After the operation of the Hindustan Paper Corporation at Jagiroad, the bamboo availability of the forests of Assam and Meghalaya are depleting at a faster rate. Further, there is an increase in the price of bamboo both in local and domestic markets. The paper mill is spreading air, water, noise and soil pollution to the surrounding villages and in the mill areas like Pachim Nagaon, Nakhula Grant, Nakhula Gaon, Jagiroad, Deosal, Bamungaon, Rawmari, Bangfor etc. The discharge of effluents of the mill, which contain toxic substances and heavy metals like calcium hydrochloride, zinc, lead, arsenic, cadmium etc., into local water bodies is continuously damaging the aquatic life. The fish population has declined and people are unwilling to take fish from the local water bodies due to the pollutants of the mill. Plant population of Mayong block is equally damaged by the pollutants. Some of the plants where the researcher finds abnormal growth are arecanut, coconut, banana and vegetable crops. The workers of the mill are exposed to different pollutants like noise, chlorine dust, formalin, vapour, metals, fumes and organic solvents. During the field study, the old people of the adjacent village of the mill reported that after the establishment of the mill, a number of diseases are common occurrence to the people.

These diseases are ulcers, cancers, cholera, hepatitis, diarrhoea, typhoid, heart problem, malaria, bronchial, asthma, upper respiratory tract infection, rhinitis, pneumonitis, fungal infection of skin, hypertension etc. Survey after survey revealed that Jagiroad is not eco-friendly and sustainable in development activities in nature due to H.P.C.

iii) *Soil Pollution*: Soil is the upper crust of the earth. The soil of Assam is acidic in reaction having ph (phosphrous content per hydrogen ion) between 4.5 and 6.5. The major groups of soil in Assam are (i) New alluvial soil, (ii) Old alluvial soil, (iii) Old mountain alluvial soil, (iv) Non-laterite red soil and (v) Laterite red soil. It was found by some research scholars that soil in many parts of Assam is steadily deteriorating in its quality and fertility due to industrial pollutants including Jagiroad area. The effluents of HPC have degraded the agricultural lands of Belguri, Deosal, Tegheria, Ghunusa etc. According to the report submitted by circle officer, Mayong Revenue Circle 1999, village-wise area of patta land affected by pollution caused by HPC are (i) Ghunusa (870 bighas), (ii) Tegheria (1359 bighas),and (iii) Deosal(300 bighas). Village-wise area of Government land affected by pollution caused by H.P.C. mill are (i) Ghunusa (80 bighas) and (ii) Tegheria (41 bighas).

iv) *Water Pollution*: The beels of Mayong Development Block are significant for flora and fauna but their biodiversity has already been threatened by HPC. The aquatic life of fisheries, beels and canals suffer due to agricultural and industrial pollution. The water quality of Jagiroad Town is poor because of industrial residues which enter into the water bodies. Often broken water pipes are contaminating the water quality of the town. There are large numbers of earthen wells at Jagiroad which get contaminated by flowing water which carries waste materials including cow-dung etc. This creates problem of safe drinking water at Jagiroad.

v) *Air pollution:* Air polluted cities of India are Ahmedabad, Bangal ore, Kolkata, Chennai, Delhi, Hyderabad, Kanpur, Lucknow, Mumbai, Nagpur and Pune. There air of Jagiroad is not safe. H.P.C. and vehicular traffic are the main causes of air pollution in Jagiroad. The are unprecedented growth of motor vehicles like two-wheelers, auto-rickshaws, taxis, mini buses, omni buses, cars, jeeps, bulldozers, buses, trucks etc. in the roads of Jagiroad. Air pollution is caused by emission of sulphur, carbon monoxide, zinc dust, smoke and intolerable smokes by automobiles. Vehicles are run by both diesel and petrol. Diesel pollution is more visible than petrol pollution. In diesel vehicles, a high degree of sulphur and carbon soot is released. In Jagiroad, old diesel vehicles continue to emit high level of suspended particulate into the atmosphere thereby contributing to air pollution. Petrol vehicles emit benzene. Benzene is a major source of air pollution besides a health hazards. It causes lung disease, lung cancer, skin cancer and leukemia. According to International Standard, benzene content in petrol in India is 5%, whereas it is 1 % in US, Japan, & European Union. Old vehicles in Jagiroad emit more pollutants than new ones. Road dust in Jagiroad contains dirt from soil and the suspended particulate matters from tail pipe emissions. Many linkage roads in Jagiroad are constructed with the waste materials supplied by H.P.C. like burnt coal, used lime and caustic. Road dust, which we inhale, is responsible for upper respiratory illness, cardio-vascular disease such as arrhythmia and cancer. It is not possible to measure the actual amount of suspendable dirt on the road. There is tremendous pressure of population in Jagiroad Town. Population pressure increased the number of vehicles in the town. The number of cycles in Jagiroad town is slowly declining because it is not safe to ride a cycle on the road. The roads of Jagiroad are choking and there is no space for expansion. Air pollution can also result a number of problem to the people like heart disease, high blood pressure and psychological disturbances.

vi) *Noise pollution*: Noise is a slow agent of death. The main sources of noise pollution at Jagiroad are the Hindustan Paper Corporation Ltd., Jagiroad, the machines used for pulling water from river and local water bodies for Boro-paddy cultivation, generator sets used during electricity failure by hotels and big business establishments and loudspeakers used in festivals. Traffic noise of Jagiroad town is caused by two-wheelers, three-wheelers, cars and trucks etc. The railway that passes through Jagiroad also causes noise pollution when the trains run both in days and nights. The other sources of noise pollution are tape recorders, record players, television sets, cinema hall, ceiling fans, hand pumps, pressure cookers, domestic generators etc. During the daytime, noise in Jagiroad town crosses the tolerable limit due to traffic noise, community noise and college/schools noise. Noise damages the cells of the ears or ruptures the eardrum. The harmful effects of noise pollution are dizziness and disorientation, ringing ears (tinnitus), insomnia, constriction of blood vessels, high blood pressure, heart disease and psychological disturbances.

vii) *Plastic Problem*: The increase use of polythene carry bags has been a cause of concern to the people of Jagiroad. Jagiroad Town is at present having plastic culture. Plastic bags contain cadmium and lead which when mixed up with food items of mass consumption cause health disorders. Already Indian Railways has passed an order to ban use of plastic cups at railway stations and trains. The Government of Tamil Nadu has banned disposable plastic cups Himachal Pradesh and Jammu & Kashmir governments have banned the use of polythene carry bags. It is essential on part of Deputy Commissioner to ban the use of plastic carry bags in the town.

Growth of Anti-Social Activities: Urbanization also promotes the growth of anti-social activities. There is phenomenal growth of this institution in the locality. Street children are gaining momentum in the area. The abnormal growth of beggary population in the township is a matter of great concern to the population of the town. There is common occurrence of thefts, dacoity and other forms of crime. Drunkard problem is also creating social disorder in the township.

Policy Recommendation: The following are the suggestions to develop Jagiroad township.

- Provision of safe drinking water to the entire inhabitants of the locality
- Setting up rain harvesting plant
- Preservation of water bodies of Jagiroad area
- H.P.C. should set up a modern Effluent Water Treatment Plant to check water pollution
- Provision of better health services
- Improvement in the drainage facilities of the area
- Improvement pothole streets of Jagiroad.
- Immediate ban on the use of caustic lime & burnt coal to fill low lying lands
- Establishments of children parks & gardens
- Establishment of electrified cremation facilities
- Establishment of public library
- Provision of better parking facilities
- Introduction of bye-lane system

- Establishment of growth centre
- Proper registration of births and deaths
- Introduction of Urban Poverty Alleviation Programme
- Slum improvement
- Establishment of community latrines and bathrooms
- Provision of better facilities to the informal sector
- Regulation in the construction of building on scientific basis
- To safeguard the interest of Tiwa community
- Conservation of Tiwa rich cultural heritage
- Preparation of Master plan for Jagiroad area
- Setting up a garbage disposal plant
- Setting up a bio-manure plant to arrest the cowdung disposal problem
- Establishing proper street lighting facilities
- Participation of NGOs and private sectors in town planning
- Allocation of sufficient resources to Jagiroad Development for proper planning
- Protection of Jagiroad environment
- Planting more eco-friendly trees.

Conclusion

Urbanization transforms the economy into a higher social and economic order. It demands better facilities on water supply, sanitation, garbage disposal, electrification, telecommunication, health services, street lights, proper housing, access to better education, transportation, playground, recreation space and so on. Therefore, a careful town planning with the provision of better amenities will provide better quality of life to the people of the township. It also requires better safeguard of the ethnic community of Jagiroad mainly Tiwa. At all cost, there should be a policy and programme to protect environment and eco- system of Jagiroad.

REFERENCES

Barman, D.K, Urban Water Problem of Guwahati City, *The Assam Tribune,* March 29, 1998.

Baruah, Alpana & Dey, Halena, *Impact of Paper Industry on Environment with Special Reference to Nagaon Paper Mill,* Jagiroad, 2004.

Bhandari, Purushottam, The Economy of Ancient Assam. International Conference on Brahmaputra Civilization, 20th and 22nd October 2000, Guwahati.

__________, Environment Problem - A Case Study of Mayong Development Block, State Level Seminar on Impact of Human Activities on Environment, 5th October 2002, Organized by Jagiroad College, Jagiroad,Morigaon (Assam) Sponsored by University Grants Commission.

__________, Environment vs. Development in Assam; Regional Seminar on the Role of Biodiversity and Environment Strategies in North-East India for Sustainable Development at St. Mary's College, Shillong, 27th & 28th November 2002.

__________, Health and Health Care (A Case Study of Mayong Development Block), International Conference on Mountain Environment and Natural Hazards Management, 27th – 29th March 2003, Organized by Department of Geography, North-Eastern Hill University, Shillong.

– – – – --, Development of Rural Enterprises and Rural Employment Generation in Assam with Special Reference to Morigaon District, 1st August 2003, Organized by Extension Education Centre, Jagiroad College, Jagiroad, Morigaon, Assam.

Cesus of India 1991, Series –4; Assam.

Census of India 2001, Series -19: Assam.

Didee, Jaymala & Rangaswamy (ed.), *Urbanization, Trends, Perspective & Challenges,* Rawat Publications, New Delhi.

Economic Survey, Assam, 2001-2002.

Economic Survey, 2002-2003.

Gautam, Hem Chandra, *Rural Development - An Integrated Approach: A Case Study of Undivided Kamrup and Darang District,* unpublished Ph.D. Thesis, 1990.

Livingstone, Lam and Goodall, A.S., *Economics and Development: An Introduction*, Oxford University Press, 1970.

Mahanta, Anjana, Urban Water Crisis, *The Assam Tribune*, Oct. 8, 2004.

Marshal, Alfred, *Principles of Economics*, Macmillan, 1930.

Sarma, Khagen, Problems Resulting from Overexploitation of Bamboos in the Neighbouring Areas of Jagiroad Paper Mill, Oct.5, 2002.

Souvenir, *Brahmaputra Beckons*, International Conference on Brahmaputra Civilization, 20t–22 Oct. 2000.

Souvenir, 22nd Biennial Conference of North- East India Geographical Society, 27th & 28th April, 2002

Statistical Hand Book Assam, 2001.

Survey of Indian Industry, 2003.

Survey of the Environment, 2000, 2001 & 2002.

Tahbildar, Munindra, Impact of Industrial Setups on the Social Economical Structure of Jagiroad Area, *Focus*, Annual Journal of Seminar Forum, Jagiroad College, Vol. 1 (2003-2004)

The World Health Report, 2002.

World Development Report, 2002.

Index

*****